CRACKING
THE CRM
CODE

HOW TO PREVENT FAILURES IN BUYING, IMPLEMENTING AND USING CRM

FOREWORD BY RASHMI BANSAL

D1800094

LIMESH PAREKH

INDIA · SINGAPORE · MALAYSIA

Notion Press

No.8, 3rd Cross Street,
CIT Colony, Mylapore,
Chennai, Tamil Nadu – 600004

First Published by Notion Press 2021
Copyright © Limesh Parekh 2021
All Rights Reserved.

ISBN 978-1-63745-468-8

Dedication

I dedicate this book to my Parents Narendra Parekh and Jyotsna Parekh. Their initials are the story behind the name of the company Enjay IT Solutions Ltd. They are no more with us, but their blessings always remain with me.

Contents

Foreword

Stay hungry, stay foolish - these were the words of Steve Jobs which inspired the title of my first book. I continue to use the phrase when I am invited to give motivational lectures and it never fails to charge up my audience. Yet, one week later that hunger feels like starvation and the foolishness has morphed into frustration. This is especially true for the SME entrepreneur.

Running a small enterprise is not easy - there are myriad issues and just one person (you, the owner) who must solve them. You are starved for time, for capital, for good people. Sitting in your office, with problems piled up on your head, you wonder - is there some tool, system or process which can make life easier? In short, you are seeking a 'brahamastra'.

You've probably heard of CRM and thought 'this isn't for me'. That is precisely why you must read this book. It doesn't expound management fundas, it doesn't use jargon. The book is wholly and solely devoted to making you - the SME entrepreneur - understand how CRM can help streamline and scale up his enterprise.

The author understands your hesitation, your pain points. He is not a salesman but a friend. Limesh has used the fiction format and unfolded the CRM story through the action and interaction of four college buddies. It makes the book readable and relatable to the aam aadmi. Pithy Hindi phrases and dialogues from popular films add to the punch.

I am especially happy to see this book being released because Limesh had attended a 2 day non-fiction writing workshop with me in September 2020. At the end of the session, many participants said they would start work on their book. But Limesh is the first to actually deliver on his promise. I hope it serves as an inspiration to many others, who are experts in their field.

To share knowledge in a manner that catches the imagination of readers.

To 'give back' to the world and rest assured, the returns will be manifold.

I wish you all the best with your book, Limesh. May it empower SMEs to grow faster, higher, stronger.

Mumbai   – **Rashmi Bansal**
15th December 2020

Preface

One should always know three things in life. क्या करना है, क्या नहीं करना है, और क्या बिलकुल नहीं करना है. *(What you should do, what you should not do, and what you should never do).*

I am a CA dropout by choice, currently CEO of a software company. I have always loved to learn and understand how organizations work. With a technology background, I could dive deeper into how technology can help organizations operate more efficiently.

But sometimes, technology alone does not help. But then we blame technology, which is convenient but erroneous.

Small businesses run the world. Technology in managing sales can help SMBs to grow faster. CRM comes with a promise to help you manage the entire customer experience, right from marketing, sales to Service.

But there is a gap; there are many challenges in buying, implementing, and using CRM. It's a complex HR and technology issue.

Hence I chose to write this book to address the issues and propose solutions. The book is divided into five chapters; (a) Deciding to buy CRM (b) Buying CRM (c) Implementing CRM (d) Getting users to use CRM (e) Growing with CRM.

We have been using CRM since 2004 and selling CRM solutions since 2009. In these eleven years, We got an opportunity to work with more than 450 companies and help them. This book is a kind of summary of that experience.

Why did I choose this topic?

There are lots of books written about CRM. Also, there is a lot of information on the internet. However, all of that information is the marketing material put by CRM vendors. It's about CRM but not about the companies who will use the CRM.

All CRM vendors tell you what their CRM software can do. But no one is telling you what you have to do. This sets the wrong expectations, and the result is a gross failure.

SMEs have different challenges as compared to large enterprises. The financial and managerial resources they have are quite limited as compared to large enterprises.

This book dives deep into the problem from the user's perspective. This is a non-fiction book written in a fiction format.

Why I chose to write in Fiction (novel) format

The learnings become very easy to understand when told in a story format. But this is not a new concept; all the Ancient Indian knowledge and wisdom has been imbibed in our stories. Maybe that is the reason why this civilization survived so long and is still thriving.

This format allows us to understand how people actually think. How leaders, bosses, owners, and other stakeholders behave. It also allows us to explore how sales teams in different industries work. What challenges they face.

Also, a fiction format allows the ideas to be easily understood. When you understand and do something, the results are fantastic. I am particularly impressed by Eliyahu Goldratt and his world-famous book ***The Goal***.

This book is about three friends and their journey with CRM. The challenges they face in this journey and how their fourth friend guides them through it. These three friends have different types and sizes of business, which they do in different ways.

There are five chapters in this book, depict different stages in the Journey of CRM.

1. Deciding to buy CRM.

2. The actual process of buying CRM.

3. Implementing CRM

4. Making your users use CRM

5. Growing your business with CRM

How did we research and write this book?

I could have written the book based on my personal experience in the last 11 years. But I wanted to write something after thorough research and study.

First, we analyzed our clients based on their usage and adoption of CRM. Then we did three rounds of feedback meetings with our clients who had more struggle with the adoption.

We also did similar meetings with our clients, who have very high adoption rates.

These two types of feedback rounds helped us to get a much better understanding of the problem and its probable solution.

Who will benefit from this book

There are three types of businesses, one that has already implemented CRM, secondly those who plan to buy CRM, third who will shortly plan to buy CRM. This book will benefit all those who run these businesses.

This book is written for small businesses. However, the ideas discussed will also apply to enterprises, but in a slightly different way.

Also, the story discussed in this book is that of B2B businesses. However, the points will be relevant for a retail business also.

Furthermore, this book will be handy for those who want to sell CRM. If sellers understand the buyer's pain and their purchase journey, it is much easier to make the sale.

Coaches and consultants who help businesses grow will also benefit from this book.

– Limesh Parekh

Acknowledgments

There is no chance I would have been able to complete this book without my family's support. By the way, I live in a joint family; we are eleven members. Ten other members include my wife, Chhaya, My brothers Chaitanya and Siddheshwar, their wives Purnima and Jaineeta, and all the kids - Shreya, Vrushali, Rohan, Yug, and Dhriti.

I also need to thank my team members at Enjay, who tolerated my absence and allowed me all the space and time. They effortlessly shouldered all my responsibilities while writing this book.

I need to mention Rashmi Bansal, author of Stay Hungry and stay foolish, for her guidance and motivation in writing this book. In fact, a non-fiction deep dive session with Rashmi motivated me to start writing a book.

A special thanks to my editor Vishal Kataria (Content Sutra), who has been a friend and a guide for me.

I have an enormous debt of gratitude to all my friends, who helped me proofread the book and provide me with valuable feedback.

1. Akarsh Mathur

2. Ishani Lad

3. Jai Bohra

4. Rajendra Panakhia

5. Sanjay Ruparel

6. Shailendra Yadav

7. Suhas Marathe

8. Taufik Patel

9. Vishal Dake

10. Vishal Patel

11. Vivek Shah

One more thanks to Pooja Dawra for a special meeting that I had with her, where she helped me visualize the book's success, which has been a strong motivation for me.

I want to acknowledge appreciation for my friend Mr. Ravindra Datar for sharing his idea on cross-selling, which has been shared in this book.

The last and the immense gratitude needs to go to all the customers of Enjay, who trusted Enjay for their CRM needs. It has been an incredible journey with all of them. Most of this book comes from the experience that I gained from them.

Chapter 1

· · · · · · · · · · · · · ·

Deciding to Buy CRM

सोच गहरी हो जाए तो फैसले कमजोर हो जाते है

– Badshah Khan, (Amitabh Bachchan)
in Khuda Gawah movie.

Liladhar Shastri took the last sip of his filter coffee as he waited for his three college buddies to join him at Madras Cafe, the same coffee shop where all four of them used to hang out. Back then, they called it their "ADDA." *(ADDA means Den, in Hindi).*

It was a rainy evening, and Liladhar was feeling a bit nostalgic. Liladhar Shastri, Anubhav Bajaj, Jagdeep Khurana, and Irshad Rangoonwala were meeting after 17 long years. Professor Ukale used to call them *'Chandal Chokdi,'* meaning the four devils.

They had done their graduation from South Indian College, Mumbai. Not only were they a bunch of naughty students, but most of the teachers did not have much hope from any of them.

But they proved their teachers were wrong in judging their competency; Today, they all are doing well in their respective businesses.

Irshad Rangoonwala

Irshad Rangoonwala, who had worked in a Multi-National Company for around a decade, always liked to plan and do things in a very systematic way.

He always aspired for corporate culture during his college days and always dreamt of working at a reputed company. However, after a decade-long corporate career with an MNC, he decided to give up his 9 to 5 job and start his own business.

Backed with more than a decade-long experience, he ventured into the distribution business of agricultural equipment in partnership with his two colleagues Pankaj Kapoor and Sanjay Khanna. They started a company in the name & style of IPS AgriTech Pvt ltd.

The Indian GDP was on the upswing, so was the agriculture sector. Indian farmers had started to modernize their farming techniques. In the last 4-5 years, they were emphasizing mechanized farming. IPS Agritech had created a distribution network in two states and employed more than 25 people. The first two years were upbeat; the founders had delivered on their idea till now and proved their merit. However, the growth came with its own perils; many investors had bet on them and now wanted to see the business scaling up at sonic speed.

Anubhav Bajaj

Anubhav belonged to a wealthy business family that owned a textile mill, and everyone expected him to carry the family legacy forward. Anubhav, however, was a dreamer and had his own vision of creating an empire based on his fascination with computers and technology. He believed he could shape the future, so armed with his gritty conviction, he set up his own business.

Anubhav's firm, R. S. Technologies, started with the traditional business of supplying IT hardware. Gradually as business prospered, Anubhav began giving shape to his dreams and diversified into IT Infra Projects and turnkey solutions. What started as one person vision now employed 180 people.

Since Anubhav belonged to a highly influential family, his business grew very fast. He was extremely successful in bagging many big-ticket and prestigious orders.

Gradually, success had its negative impact on Anubhav. He wanted to delegate more than what his team was ready for, which caused him to doubt their capabilities. He was not happy with his team, which had got him the initial success. He felt his team should drive the company's future growth while he could enjoy the perks of entrepreneurship and his early success. Golf courses replaced meeting rooms and long leisure holidays became more frequent than business trips.

He resented his line managers & openly doubted their capabilities. In his opinion, they lacked any will to take responsibility.

Jagdeep Khurana

In contrast, Jagdeep took up the mantle of his family business within a year of graduation and filled in the void created because of his father's untimely demise. A company dealing in imported industrial gears that his father had painstakingly established.

Young but inexperienced, Jagdeep managed everything calmly. Whenever seeds of doubts erupted in his mind, he had the unwavering support from his better half, Jaspreet, to help him clear his mind and continue his journey.

In his office, he had around ten people and more than 20 workers in his workshop.

Jagdeep Khurana was the polar opposite of Anubhav Bajaj. He was always well aware of all aspects of his business but with a conservative mindset, while Anubhav was unabashedly ambitious and reckless.

Jagdeep believed in being overly hands-on and always insisted on perfection. Anything less than 100% was not an option for his team. As a result, he often found himself drowned in mundane work that could be easily delegated. He was never happy with what his team did.

Liladhar Shastri

Liladhar Shastri proudly told everyone that he had been an outstanding student throughout his school life, but with a difference. He was always standing outside the classroom because teachers punished him regularly.

It was not that Liladhar was not smart. But somehow, the subjects taught in the school and the teaching method always bored him.

Liladhar came from a family of accountants and teachers. No one in his family ever ventured into business. But Liladhar had completely different plans.

Narrottam Shastri, Liladhar's father, had a dream that Liladhar should become a Chartered Accountant. Like an obedient son, Liladhar pursued CA and passed out with good marks.

Along with his Chartered Accountancy studies, he took up part-time account writing jobs.

This was the time when India was opening up to the possibilities in the world of computers. Liladhar was fascinated by Tally, the Accounting Package.

Mesmerized by the efficiency of the software, Liladhar switched to Software engineering as a career. He runs a Software development company from a small town (more of a village than a town.)

Liladhar Shastri was the bluntest and most outspoken person in this gang.

Lately, he had joined a course on Ayurved and Yog in Mumbai.

The Meeting

Liladhar was going through all that they had discussed over the phone in the last few months.

His chain of thoughts broke as he saw an identifiable face at the entrance of Madras Cafe. It was Irshad. Time had been very harsh with his hair, but he was fit and smiling as ever. Back in college, too, Irshad was fond of sports and exercise. He had a glowing face and a wide toothy grin, which showed up prominently on his face because of his dark skin.

A big fan of Amitabh Bachchan, Irshad enjoyed it when all his friends called him *'Kaalia,'* an iconic character Amitabh Bachchan played in a blockbuster movie.

Liladhar waved at him. "Hi Liladhar, you have not changed much. Even now, you are as chubby as you were back in college." Liladhar replied mischievously, "Kaalia, even you have not changed. But unfortunately, now you cannot audition for a shampoo ad!!"

Just as they were settling down after a warm hug, Jagdeep showed up. "Where is your *Judwa?*" exclaimed Irshad and Liladhar with a twinkle in their eyes.

Jagdeep and Anubhav were not twin brothers, but they were close friends in school and college. Together they both hatched mischievous adventures to the extent that teachers could not even imagine. Such was their bonding that everybody called them *'Judwa.' (Judwa, in Hindi, means twins.)*

"He might be *stuck in the traffic,* as usual. His patent excuse for arriving late," Jagdeep said.

Like in college, Anubhav was always in a hurry but always late. "Anyways, we can order, and he'll join us soon," Jagdeep added.

After almost 15 minutes, Anubhav arrived in his black S class Mercedes. As he stepped out from the back seat of his car, people stopped to look at this man who looked debonair in his branded suit, aviator goggles, and swanky watch.

"We all know you got stuck in traffic," Irshad said. To that, Jagdeep added, "As usual."

Anubhav started cribbing about his business as he was settling in. "No *yaar,* our business is such that we are always late. Our customers are always unreasonable and demanding, and because of fierce competition, we have to give in."

For almost 30 minutes, they were immersed in the pleasant memories of school and college days. They also shared their experiences on how their life had been a rollercoaster ride.

"Liladhar, what makes you interested in Ayurveda and Yoga? And how do you find so much time from your busy schedule? Doesn't your business suffer?" Anubhav asked, who always complained of being overworking.

"Firstly, it's Ayurved and Yog, not Ayurveda and Yoga. When we take so much care to pronounce English words correctly, we must not do injustice to our own words!" Liladhar corrected him.

Anubhav realized his mistake but did not like to accept it, "hmm."

Irshad added, "Yes, buddy, we all would like to know that. We understand that you have a team of 50+ people working in your organization, My team is 25 people, and Jagdeep's team is just ten people; we are keen to know your secret, it will be useful for us when we grow our business". To which, Jagdeep nodded.

Irshad added, "For the first two years when my partners and I were hands-on, we were sailing through comfortably, but then as we have started to grow, we have started facing headwinds.."

Jagdeep tried to explain his perspective. "Maybe that is because you always worked in a large corporate world where everything is systematic, and there is an SOP (Specified Operating Procedure) for everything, but managing a smaller organization is all together with a different game."

"Maybe that is true," Irshad said. "We are struggling to anticipate & resolve these challenges to scale our business eventually. The market potential is huge, but we are bogged down in just getting through our existing setup & unable to scale."

"That is the usual problem," Liladhar jumped in. "You have a lot of ideas and strategies but struggle with implementation. This is more true in the case of people who have worked within a corporate culture and then start their own business."

Then he turned to Anubhav and said, "I understand that both Jagdeep and Irshad have smaller teams, but you have a quite large team. What keeps you busy then?"

Now it was Anubhav 's turn to bring out his frustration. "Leave it *yaar*. Even with a huge team, I have to do all the running. My managers are inefficient. And the senior people are so egoistic that I cannot tell them anything forcefully." He also added, "that is the reason I want to know, how do you handle these responsibilities?"

"If you think that having a larger team will make you free, you are wrong. With increased team size, the complexity of business increases, and our responsibilities also increase, we are juggling more balls" Anubhav brought out his real frustration.

Liladhar said, "See, we have first to understand that as entrepreneurs, **we have to play multiple roles of being owner, manager as well as executive**. Generally, the executive in us takes preference, which is completely wrong. We have to understand that we are owners first and then executives."

Jagdeep argued, "Yes, but the entire business is our responsibility, and we cannot rely entirely on our employees."

"No, everything is not our responsibility. There are only two responsibilities of an entrepreneur," Liladhar clarified.

"Only two?" Jagdeep was shocked. "And would you mind explaining to us which two?"

1. Two Fundamental responsibilities of any business owners

"**Fundamentally, the only two responsibilities of a business owner are Marketing and Innovation. We can delegate everything else to our team members**." Liladhar Shastri said as if revealing some grand secret.

However, this left his friends more confused. Jagdeep said, one-word "Explain."

"See, when we all started our businesses, we kept meeting people and doing whatever we could do to create visibility and generate sales. Also, we kept putting in a lot of effort to learn and improve our way of doing things. In fact, we were fine-tuning everything as often as possible." Liladhar explained.

"Yes, that is marketing and innovation," Jagdeep said.

"However, when our business started to grow, we settled for a good chair and a nice cabin. We just sat in the office. What were we doing? We looked after invoices, deliveries, payment collections, monitoring our staff, and just making sure that everything works as it is. Improvement or innovation is lost. And we also lost our contact with the customer. We were no more the face of our organization."

Irshad nodded. "This is exactly my story, and I am sure Jagdeep and Anubhav are also going through the same. In fact, all Small Business Owners are going through the same. But then what is the solution? Our teams are not capable enough to be delegated with all the responsibilities."

"How do you implement processes, and how do you make sure that your team is following everything? How do you make your business run smoothly without you?" Anubhav was as curious as a cat now.

"It's all about policy, process, and culture," Liladhar replied. "But before we talk more, let us order something to eat. Also, I hope Madras Cafe remains open till late at night, and you guys are OK staying late."

Two primary responsibilities of Business Owners.

Fundamentally, there are only two responsibilities of a business owner—Marketing and Innovation. Owners can delegate everything else.

2. Aligning Policy, Process, and Culture

"We have created policies and even hired a professional agency to create documents for us, but every policy is just dead weight in our computer files and also on our notice boards," Anubhav complained.

Jagdeep had a different problem. "We don't even have time and bandwidth to create policy documents. This idea would not be useful for us."

"Let me tell you one thing. Do not blindly start implementing everything mentioned in the management books. Use your common sense first," Liladhar said sternly. "First, understand the concept and relationship between policy, process, and culture and evaluate how it will impact your company. Let me give you an example."

"Yes, that would help," Anubhav said.

Learnings from The No parking Sign

"Let's say there is a **No Parking** sign on the road. It's a policy, right? But no one is following that policy (or instructions). This means that policy is present, but the process is absent," Liladhar explained.

"How can you say that the process is absent? There is a rule that if I park the car, I have to pay a fine," Irshad argued.

"Exactly! That's also just a policy, and it's not getting implemented," Liladhar continued. "What do we need to do to get this implemented?"

"Simple. Depute a police officer there. Everybody will follow the process." Irshad had a prompt answer.

"Perfect, which means now we have both - policy and process. What will happen if we remove that policeman because having a policeman under every no-parking sign is not possible?" Liladhar countered back.

"That is exactly what's happening in our organizations. We implement but do not enforce it through regular follow-up and eventually what started as a promising new policy, fizzles out and ends up as just another policy nos in our files." Irshad nodded his head in utter disappointment.

"This means if people start following the process without a policeman, it would mean the presence of culture?" Now Anubhav was already ahead in the thought process. "But the real problem is, how do we achieve that?"

"The first step towards building a culture is to create a policy. Then have a monitoring mechanism. You should continue the monitoring till you feel the process has been ingrained in the daily routine, and thus culture has been established," Liladhar explained.

"Also, bringing in the culture has a lot of logic behind it. But let us simplify it. Do you remember the way you taught me cycling when we were in the 5th standard?" Liladhar asked Anubhav.

"What? Anubhav taught you cycling?" Irshad asked because he had joined the gang much later in the 9th standard.

"Yes, and believe me, it was challenging to teach him. He can be a difficult student. He could not manage a simple cycle; god knows how is he managing this business?" Anubhav winked.

"Yes, and I fondly appreciate the patience shown by Anubhav in teaching me cycling over those five weeks. I took five long weeks to learn cycling." Liladhar explained with acceptance on his face.

"Ok, but what's the point?" Irshad was impatient.

"Once Anubhav got me on the cycle, I simply could not figure out where to focus and what to do. Should I look at the handle, to begin with, or should I peddle? At that time, Anubhav held my seat and handle, and literally pushed me, and helped me balance. He would manage my entire weight and also push me forward. Poor Anubhav." Liladhar continued.

"Yes, but if I had let you loose, you would have definitely fallen," Anubhav replied.

"After a few challenging days, I could manage the peddling part, but still, the balance was a problem. So now Anubhav was running with me, he did not have to push me, but still had to grab my handle and hold my entire balance," said Liladhar.

"Perhaps in the third week, I was able to kind of manage the handle also, but still Anubhav had to run along with me, occasionally holding my handle and nudging me back on track. I think in the fourth week, I was on my own. But Anubhav still ran behind me to make sure that I didn't crash," Liladhar said with a sense of gratitude towards Anubhav.

"It was only in the fifth week that I could stand in the middle of the ground and watch your cycle. But even in the fifth week, you fell twice," Anubhav remembered with a goofy smile.

"Yes, that was the last time I crashed. Thanks to you, now I often go on 50-100 km rides with my friends," Liladhar said.

"Ok, ok, but how do we use this idea for implementing process and culture in our business," said Jagdeep as he tried to bring the focus back to the point being discussed.

"You have to teach your team members cycling. Not literally, of course. You have to handhold them till they understand how to do it on their own. Even after they are on their own, you must still keep an eye on them to make sure they do not wander off the track and crash," Liladhar explained.

"How long do you think it would take us to teach 'cycling' to our team?" Irshad enquired. He initially thought that the problem was with his team, but now it was finally dawning on him that his own approach could be the reason things were not how he wanted them to be.

"My yog teacher says that it takes 21 days of daily practice to form a habit and 42 days of daily practice to make it our second nature. I hope that answers your question." Liladhar explained, expecting some agreement from his three friends.

"So, is that how you made your team self-reliant? Can they function without your daily supervision?" Jagdeep was eager to reconfirm.

"Yes, but still, I have to oversee and guide them when required. I dedicate 20 minutes daily for complete tracking and coordination." Liladhar explained.

 Policy, process, and culture.

Creating policies is simple, but it will require proper training and supervision to convert that policy into a process. However, the ultimate goal is to have a culture where procedures are followed even without supervision.

"Just 20 minutes? It seems like you might be having a very comprehensive and exhaustive system that can manage everything. Which ERP system have you installed?" Anubhav was curious to know.

"No. A comprehensive ERP system is an overkill for small companies like ours. We use Tally for managing inventory, accounts, and finance, and a CRM system to manage Sales and Service."

Now, Anubhav had already failed to implement two different CRM systems, so he was more surprised. "But, why on earth are you using two systems? Can't you get one good ERP that will have CRM modules also?" He enquired.

3. The Difference between A CRM & ERP

"That is the biggest mistake that people make. The difference is much greater." Liladhar continued. "*The fundamental purpose of an ERP is to measure money and material, and that of a CRM tool is to manage processes and people*. Of course, they overlap in many scenarios. But their fundamental purposes are different."

"That is the reason we do not see any ERP company having great CRM software. Even those who use the best ERPs still get a dedicated CRM system to ensure all aspects are well-taken care of. Similarly, many CRM companies have tried to develop inventory and accounts modules, but they have rarely succeeded." Liladhar added.

"An ERP focuses on a post-mortem. It analyses things that have happened. A CRM tool, on the other hand, focuses on anticipating things like your Funnel, your sales forecast, and your receivables."

"But these companies do not tell us that in their advertisements or sales pitch," Anubhav said angrily.

"They have to sell, and the easiest way of selling is to take advantage of customers' lack of understanding. I think it's the buyers' fault. They should do a thorough search and study," Liladhar looked surprised. "इतने मासूम कैसे हो सकते हो." *(How can you be so innocent?)*

 CRM & ERP are different.

CRM & ERP have a very different philosophy and psychology. The Fundamental purpose of ERP is to MEASURE money and material, whereas CRM tries to MANAGE people and processes related to customer experience.

"Do you think I need a CRM? It's Ok for Anubhav and Irshad; in comparison, my company with just a ten people team, including my wife and me, is small," Jagdeep asked.

4. Does my company need a CRM?

Are we too small for CRM?

"Size does not matter. We implemented CRM when we were a five-member team," Liladhar said. "On the other side, I know many companies which have grown to more than 250-300 crores, but they are still not using CRM."

"The need for a CRM tool does not depend on your size or your turnover. It depends on two things: your sales cycle and your sales value. Moreover, it's a matter of management foresight to have CRM or not." Liladhar explained.

"Explain," Jagdeep said again, sensing a solution to his long-standing problem.

Liladhar took a paper napkin and started to draw on it. "Let's create a quadrant to understand it. On one axis, we will put the sales value, and on the other, we will put the ease of sales.

"To make things simple, we will consider low-value sales and high-value sales, on one axis," Liladhar said.

"On the other axis, we consider a simple sale and complex sales. Simple sales where the steps in the sales process are between 1-3. A single meeting or a single call sale is a simple sale." Liladhar started to explain as if he was a professor of some Oxford college.

He had drawn a diagram something like this:

"Now, if you have simple and low-value sales, you do not need a CRM software. It's like our *panwala* or someone selling SIM cards," Liladhar explained.

"Yes, it's obvious. But it became clear only when you drew this. I am excited. I want to see where my business falls," Jagdeep said, enchanted with the new enlightenment.

"If you have complex and low-value sales, then you need a CRM tool because your sales process is complex, but maybe you might not be able to afford it because of low margins," Liladhar said.

"In fact, if the sales process is complex with lower sales values and margins, a business might not survive for long. Or it will struggle for margins," Liladhar explained.

"Ok, I get it. I was wondering what kind of businesses fall under this category? Maybe computer hardware resellers will be one example. I can tell that because we are part of that industry," Anubhav said. "We can survive because we have ventured into newer technologies like security and Cloud projects; otherwise, it would have been tough for us,"

"*You make money in technology only twice. Either when it is very new or when it is fairly outdated.* By the way, this is applicable for most businesses," Liladhar interrupted Anubhav before continuing his story.

"The third quadrant has companies with high value and simple sales. Take a jewelry shop or a high-end consumer durable goods as an example. They need a CRM tool but can work without it as long as they do business in one location with the owner sitting in the shop." Liladhar explained.

"Won't an Apple store also come into that category?" Anubhav argued.

"Yes, but as the Apple franchise grows to multiple stores, it has to implement the CRM system because of other benefits of CRM tools," Liladhar added.

"Which other benefits?" Jagdeep asked curiously. He wanted reasons to justify the decision to convince his wife, who was a partner in the business.

"Let us finish the fourth quadrant first, and then I will give your answer. So, finally, the companies that have complex, high-value sales should have a CRM. It's a must for them. As the cost of lost opportunity is much higher in that case," Liladhar explained, "Most of the B2B companies will fall under this category."

"According to this, we need a CRM tool," Jagdeep said, but he still wanted more reasons to conclude the CRM buying decision.

"What if the sale is coming from only a few customers or a job work company. Do they also need a CRM tool?" Jagdeep asked.

"No, in that case, they do not need a CRM tool, at least for the sales process. But they might need one for the service management, or complaint or Helpdesk management as it is generally called," Liladhar explained.

"We are waiting to listen to the other reasons that you referred to for buying CRM," Jagdeep was as curious as a child to hear those answers.

"See, sales management is an imperfect science. All other departments, like production and accounting, have standards. But there are no such standards in sales management. So it is a great idea to have a CRM system in place and get the sales process implemented correctly." Liladhar said.

"Of course, the most important of the benefits of CRM can be having usable information about your (past, present, and future) customers so that you can do cross-selling," Liladhar added. "Finally, CRM adds that missing efficiency and rhythm to your sales team."

"*One last thing*, as Steve Jobs used to say, If you are planning to go public or raise funding, then a CRM tool is a must. Because your accounts will only show what you have already done, but your CRM will show how you are doing it. No doubt, Merchant Bankers and Private Equity Investors love companies that use CRM and follow a process." Liladhar concluded.

"Yes, I agree. That's why we have struggled with a CRM tool two times, as we intend to raise capital. Even our consultant had advised us that. But unfortunately, we have not succeeded," Anubhav confessed.

Jagdeep & Irshad were in a dilemma. They had understood that their company needed a CRM tool but had one burning question in their minds. "Isn't a CRM tool costly?"

Do you need a CRM?

Are you working IN your business or ON your business? If you want a System-driven and process-oriented organization, then CRM is a must. Of course, another way is that you can keep on working and doing all the supervision yourself.

5. But CRM is too costly

Compare Gym Subscription with CRM Software

"Do you go to the Gym?" Liladhar asked all three of them. Irshad replied that he was regular. Of all four of the friends, Irshad was always physically active right from the early days.

Now Liladhar and Irshad both looked at Anubhav and Jagdeep. Both of them never went to the Gym. "I don't have time for it even though I realize that it's important that I take care of my health," Anubhav said. "I even paid for the Gym twice but never went after the first week."

"I think it's a waste of time & money. I do some Pranayam and Yogasans at home and also go for a walk in the nearby park every morning, along with Jaspreet," Jagdeep said.

Now Liladhar had found his protagonist to take ahead his example. "Anubhav, you are right. You might think that the money to be paid to Gym is an absolute waste because you did not use it." Liladhar said. " The same is the case with CRM software; the primary reason why people feel it's costly is that they do not put in enough effort to implement it properly."

Two types of CRM Costs

"There are two types of costs involved in implementing a CRM tool: the direct cost and the Indirect cost. Direct costs are the amount of money we

pay to a CRM vendor, including subscription, implementation, training, customization, and integration costs. Indirect costs are the resources we must invest in training, changing habits, implementing the processes, managing changes in the reporting style, etc." Liladhar explained.

"Moreover, the Indirect cost of CRM is generally much higher than the direct costs. Many times it happens that people who negotiate hard on the direct cost fail to lower the indirect costs." Liladhar explained.

Our Salary bill and CRM costs

"There is also one more justification for CRM costs. You currently pay Rs. 5 lacs as your monthly salary expenses to your staff. With your current way of working, are you getting the full value of the same?" Liladhar asked.

"Sort of. However, it requires lots of effort from our side, and I'm sure Irshad and Anubhav also have the same scenario," Jagdeep said.

"Do you think that the efficiency of your team will improve if there is a proper CRM system implemented and used by your team members, including you?" Liladhar threw the second question.

"Of course," the three of them replied unanimously.

"Ok, How much of an increase do you expect," Liladhar asked.

"Maybe 50 percent," Irshad said.

"I think 25-30 percent would be achievable, provided we use it perfectly," Anubhav corrected Irshad. Jagdeep agreed with Anubhav.

"Can you do similar managerial efforts without the CRM platform and still get the results? I mean, can you achieve efficiency in your Sales and service teams without a CRM tool?" Liladhar asked.

"Absolutely not! The CRM tool will form the technology backbone and framework for the organization to work efficiently," Anubhav replied.

"Ok, let's say you will get only an efficiency increase of 20%. Does a CRM tool, which will cost 5% of your Salary costs, justify itself?" Liladhar asked.

"Oh, I see. I never thought of it this way. But Yes, I am convinced with this approach," Irshad agreed. "But we have to put proper efforts to use and implement it properly."

 Is CRM costly?

CRM is costly only if we don't use it. Also, we should consider it as a necessary HR expenditure. Why do we provide Tea/Coffee or chair for our team members to work? To increase employee productivity. Right? CRM also comes in the same category.

"Now, we need to search for a CRM specific for our Industry. We are into the distribution of Agriculture tools. Do you know of any specific CRM Vendors that make one for Agri-distribution Industry? Because I could not find one." Irshad said.

6. Should we buy CRM specific to our Industry?

"Generally, all CRM platforms are designed to be Industry-agnostic, which means a CRM tool can work in any company regardless of the industry. Unless in specific cases like Banking and retail. Otherwise, all the companies can use the same CRM software, with minimal tweaking," Liladhar explained.

"Please explain," Jagdeep was still confused.

"All the sales processes are similar. You get an inquiry; then you follow up with that inquiry in different ways. You call, meet, send emails and messages, give Demos arrange for technical discussions or POC (proof of concept), and then send the proposal and, finally, there is negotiation and closure of the sales. Almost any CRM can do this." Liladhar said everything in one big breath.

Irshad had a big question. "But what about our processes and our way of working. Will any CRM be fit for us?"

"Not any, but most of CRM will fit," Liladhar said. "Also, most of us like to believe that what we are doing is very special. In fact, it is not. We all do almost the same thing, with slight differences. So do not worry about CRM for specific industries."

"In that case, any CRM can manage complaints and tickets. Am I correct?" Jagdeep asked.

"Yes, but in our business, we also have maintenance contracts with our Customers. I hope that also can be managed?" Anubhav asked.

Now Anubhav, who had already unsuccessfully experienced two CRM software till now, jumped in. "Bhai, everything is there in most of the CRM packages; our people just have to use it properly."

"Right, you don't need to look for your Industry-specific CRM unless you find some CRM prominently popular in your industry," Liladhar explained.

Jagdeep added, "Yes, ultimately, CRM is a reporting tool, so if we use it properly, it will give proper results."

"You are wrong. This is the biggest mistake that people make," Liladhar said.

"Which one? Jagdeep asked.

"Most people think of a CRM tool as a reporting tool. It's not for bosses or team leaders," Liladhar said. "Most of the old School management ideas are focused on a top-down approach—that of command and control. Of course, a CRM tool will help you with the reporting. But that is not its primary purpose."

Jagdeep said his favorite word, "Explain, please."

"A CRM tool should help everyone in the team. It should help them to carry out their roles with clarity and ease," Liladhar seemed to be enjoying himself. "All new and modern CRM systems are designed with users in mind and not the bosses."

"Maybe this is the primary reason why our two previous adventures failed,"

Anubhav added. "We were obsessed with MIS and reporting."

 Industry-Specific CRM?

Generally, the Sales process for any B2B business is quite similar to the CRM perspective. Any good CRM will be able to handle it. No need to search for Industry-specific CRM. But it's a good idea to talk to some Industry people who are using CRM.

---

7. CRM or no CRM - The Conclusion

"Phew, there are lots of questions, which are yet to be answered. Will we be able to implement CRM properly?" Jagdeep asked, doubtfully.

"Don't worry; we have Liladhar to guide us at every stage. He has already done it successfully," Anubhav added.

Just then, the hotel boy came and suggested that now he has to close the place.

All the four friends decided to meet after 15 days, as Liladhar would be coming to the city again for his next Yog and Ayurved Class.

"Do you remember the movie "*Khuda Gawah*," starring Amitabh Bachchan?" Liladhar asked.

"How can you forget Sridevi? She was the heroine," Irshad, who had a massive crush on Sridevi, said.

"Oh, Yes, but today I want you to remember something else," Liladhar added. "My all-time favorite dialogue from all the Amitabh Bachchan Movies."

"सोच गहरी हो जाए तो फ़ैसले कमजोर हो जाते हैं" (*Too much of thinking will weaken your decision.*). *- Liladhar.*

Useful Info: List of reasons to buy a CRM tool

You need a CRM tool in the following scenarios:

1. The Sales Cycle is longer than one call or one meeting.

2. The ticket size (single sale value) is sizable.

3. Your sales team consists of more than three people.

4. You want to make your organization system-driven and process-oriented.

5. The product or service demands after-sales service. A CRM tool will help to manage Complaints.

6. There is a possibility of customers making multiple purchases. A CRM tool simplifies cross-selling and upselling.

7. You want to work ON the business and not IN the business.

When you do not need a CRM tool:

1. When few clients give repeat business.

2. When you own a single retail shop (not a multi-location retail business)

3. When the sales cycle and ticket value are small.

4. When you're sure, the business will never grow big.

Chapter 2

Actual Process of Buying CRM

सही बात को सही वक़्त पे किया जाए तो उसका मज़ा ही कुछ और होता है

— *Vijay Kumar (Amitabh Bachchan),*
in Trishul, Movie

It had been fifteen days since their last meeting. Now Irshad, Liladhar, Jagdeep, and Anubhav were meeting again. This time, it was in the office of Anubhav Bajaj since he had a large office with a spacious conference room.

In their last meeting, all three friends had decided that they needed a CRM tool, and they would initiate the buying process.

Fortunately, this time, everyone was there before the time, as they were super excited about the discussion.

Even some of Anubhav's team members had joined the meeting. They had queries and wanted to get answers for those.

One of them was Shankar Narayan, the CTO of R. S. Technologies, for the last seven years.

Shankar had many doubts he needed to be cleared since the previous CRM implementation had failed. He had been pivotal in the earlier adventures of RS Technologies with the CRM. He was curious to participate in the discussion.

"Anubhav told me that now we are planning to implement a CRM tool again. This time we are determined to make it successful. I am sure your experience and guidance will help us," Shankar told Liladhar.

"I have a few questions. We have tried implementing CRM two times before also. But we have not been successful," Shankar complained."In both cases, we selected reputed MNC brands of CRM and spent heavily on the customization. But unfortunately, we failed every time." Shankar continued.

"Our team is not interested in doing data entry in the system. Our team members do not want any reporting tool to succeed," Shankar continued, with more disappointment.

"Tell me one thing, who were the team members involved in the decision making of the process of buying the CRM and customizing it," Liladhar asked.

Anubhav interrupted in-between "Since Shankar is CTO of the company, he looks after all the technology deployments in our organization. So, he had taken demos and designed all the customization."

"Don't mind, but this is one of the most common mistakes people make," Liladhar clarified.

1. Who should make the CRM buying decision?

"CRM is not a technology decision, but a management decision," Liladhar said.

Jagdeep said his favorite term, "Explain, please."

"As we discussed in our last meeting, a CRM tool is supposed to help managers and executives. If it's a Sales CRM, then it should focus on helping Sales Managers and Sales Executives" - Liladhar.

"Yes, I know that. But these people do not know anything about CRM technology." Shankar replied.

"They are supposed to know their work, which is Sales and Sales Management. CRM vendors need to understand technology. We can focus on the benefits of the same," Liladhar explained.

"But while deciding on a CRM, we need to understand complex things like Database, reporting, API, integrations, and other things. How can we decide without that knowledge," Shankar argued?

"You are absolutely right. Of course, technology is important. You cannot end up buying old and obsolete solutions. Also, it has to be scalable," Liladhar agreed.

"But, I still maintain that it is a business decision and not a technology decision. I can tell that with my experience," Liladhar said with authority.

"Ok, tell me one thing. Are your salespeople using mobile and WhatsApp?" asked Liladhar.

"Of course," Shankar replied, a little surprised at this silly question.

"Then they know enough technology to adapt to CRM when proper training for the process and software is given," Liladhar explained.

"Did we analyze the challenges of our Sales team members? Even our Sales Managers will have challenges; we have to consider them also," Liladhar said.

"We do not get accurate reports for analysis. Hence we are not sure," Shankar explained.

"We do not need reports for those. We just need to observe the way our team works. Have face-to-face meetings with them. Listen to their stories about the success and failures," Liladhar added.

"Did you ever attend any sales review meetings?" Liladhar turned to Shankar and asked.

"No, I am a Chief Technical Officer, So I don't attend Sales review meetings. I understand what you are trying to say. But most of our large customers also take technology decisions the same way," Shankar answered, somewhat defensively.

"That is another big mistake that Small Businesses make. See, a small company cannot function exactly like a big company. In fact, the systems and processes of a large company will only break the smaller teams" - Liladhar.

"I agree that a technology person needs to be involved in the CRM Buying process. But the primary decision-makers need to be the Functional team." Liladhar added

"There is also another hidden benefit of involving the functional team. It initiates acceptance of the new idea, which will result in better user adoption and CRM usage. -Liladhar.

Jagdeep added, "I think Liladhar is right. Buying a CRM tool is not a technological decision."

 Buying CRM is a management decision.

Always include the Sales and Service team leaders and members while deciding the requirements of a CRM tool. The IT team can guide you, but it should not make the buying decision.

"In fact, there is a difference between active and passive technologies here. When we buy an email server or a firewall, although people benefit from it, they don't use it directly and regularly," Liladhar said.

"Whereas with business applications like CRM and ERP software, people have to interact with them. Their way of working will change significantly because of these software platforms." Liladhar's explanation seemed to convince them.

But not all of them.

"But can you explain how you take that decision in your organization?" Anubhav asked. Anubhav had realized there was something fundamentally wrong in what they had done before.

40

"When we implemented a CRM tool, like 16 years ago, in 2004, there were only five people on the team. Three brothers, one of my cousins, and one peon." Liladhar explained.

"I looked after the sales with one more person who helped me with back-office work. Two people took care of product development and customer support. The peon took care of deliveries and other stuff" - added Liladhar.

"Since I played the role of a Salesperson and Sales Manager, I knew how we were selling and what I needed to do as a sales manager," Liladhar said.

"So it was almost our entire team who participated in the planning the requirements for the CRM," Liladhar said.

"What about the support team? Who represented them?" Jagdeep asked.

"Both the team members who were handling product development and customer support joined the meetings and decision making," Liladhar explained.

Anubhav interrupted, "But that is when you were a small team. What about little larger teams like ours?"

Shankar added, "Also, our Sales team is jam-packed meeting their Sales targets and fulfilling their role. I don't think they could have spared the time for the same."

"I have observed in many organizations that change is left to the juniors while seniors maintain the status quo," Liladhar said while confusing everyone in the room.

Jagdeep raised his usual request, "Explain, please."

"Let me tell you something about my company. We have a proverbial policy which goes something like this: नए धंधे में पुराना आदमी चाहिए, पुराने धंधे में नया आदमी चलेगा." Liladhar said.

"Which movie was this dialogue in?" Irshad asked as he could not recollect the dialogue from any Indian movie.

"No, this is not from any movie. It is our internal policy. Whenever we try anything new, a product, a process, or a policy, we always get our most senior people involved in it," Liladhar explained.

"What's the benefit in it? In fact, it's the contrary. We have always seen companies get new teams for new products, and they don't disturb their existing teams." Jagdeep was not only curious but also confused.

"Yes, because those big companies get experts from the Industry to form a new team, whereas smaller companies like us don't have experts. We have juniors." Liladhar explained.

"Agreed, But.. " Jagdeep started.

"See, the senior person knows companies' goals, processes, challenges, market conditions, and lots of other experience," Liladhar interrupted. "This helps them to handle new situations in a better way."

"One more benefit is that when seniors drive the things, juniors follow quickly. Whereas the other way around does not work," Liladhar explained.

"In fact, this can apply to the customers and products also. When we want to sell any new product, first try your existing customers. Since they trust you, the chances of them buying will be much more, as compared to strangers." Anubhav had got the idea.

"नया product बेचने के लिए, पुराने ग्राहक के पास जाओ, और नए ग्राहक को वो product बेचो जो आप बहुत वक्त से बेच रहे हो (If you want to sell a new product, approach an old customer, and approach new customers with the products you've been selling since long)," Jagdeep said as if he was delivering dialogue in a film.

"Wow, Jagdeep, Now I think you have got it."

Golden Rule of Business.

नए धंधे में पुराना आदमी चाहिए, पुराने धंधे में नया आदमी चलेगा.
You need Senior team members for new tasks (or business). But in existing (old) tasks (or business), you may deploy new team members.

"However, there is one more reason why your senior team members are not participating in the CRM buying exercise," Liladhar blasted one more bomb.

"They consider that a CRM tool is not for them, that it won't help them. They consider that this is a new reporting tool deployed by the top management to TRACK them." Liladhar said.

"We need to consider CRM as a tool which is going to increase the efficiency and effectiveness of the sales team." Liladhar continued.

Anubhav tried to conclude, "It means that we need to involve our functional teams for the decision making of buying CRM."

"Yes, at least the team leaders and some of the senior executives," Liladhar added to his conclusion.

"Let me tell you my story." Jagdeep also wanted answers to his challenges.

"In our case, my wife, Jaspreet, who is also with me in the business, has already started taking trials of a few CRM solutions," Jagdeep said.

"Same here," Irshad added. "In our case, we have Sugandha, a new Management Graduate who has joined us as an intern, is taking the trials."

"I have a powerful feeling that the CRM trials do not work for a large number of cases. There are genuine reasons for that," - Liladhar interrupted Jagdeep.

2. Why do CRM trials not work?

Jagdeep asked his favorite question: "Explain. Please?"

"Ok, tell me what is the role of your wife, Jaspreet, in your organization," Liladhar asked Jagdeep.

"She looks after accounts and purchases," Jagdeep replied.

"Exactly, she is not looking after Sales; she might not be fully aware of the challenges that your Sales team faces. I suppose the sales team reports to you, right?" Liladhar asked Jagdeep again.

"Yes, she does not know much about the sales process and sales management, except sales figures," Jagdeep added.

Jagdeep continued, "Now, I think I understand why she could not take the decision even after taking trials for the last two weeks."

"Irshad, how much does Sugandha know about your sales process and how your sales team works?" Liladhar asked.

"Next to nothing," Irshad replied.

"Also, has Jaspreet or Sugandha, any of them, used a CRM software before?" Liladhar again asked both of them. To which both of them replied negatively. However, their facial expression revealed that both of them had understood the flaw in their approach.

"Let me summarise this for all of you. Generally, CRM trial is done by people who are least associated with the Sales process or the service process for that matter." - Liladhar.

"Further, most of the time, people in charge of taking trials have not used CRM themselves previously. So, no previous experience of handling a team who was using CRM." Liladhar added.

Liladhar continued, "What do you think they will check and try when they do not know the (Sales) process as well as the (CRM) software?"

Shankar replied, "Obviously, they can still look for the user-friendliness of the software."

"Right. But on what basis?" Liladhar asked.

"Looks and UI (User Interface) are the only things that they can check. I suppose," Anubhav answered.

"Exactly. But that does not make sure that they will succeed in their task of choosing the right CRM for your team." Liladhar said.

Shankar added to this, "We had asked our sales team to try out the software. We had specially requested multiple login IDs from the vendor. But unfortunately, they did not care even to check the same."

"We even extended the trial period from 14 days to 45 days. But still, that did not make any difference. They just don't want to do anything." Shankar complained.

"No, I don't think it's their fault. A CRM tool is not a generic mobile app like WhatsApp or some tool like Excel. These are general-purpose tools. In contrast, CRM will be managing your business processes. It will be configured to manage the processes." Liladhar said.

"That explains why companies spend millions on the user adoption but still can't achieve it," Liladhar explained.

"How can we expect that they will try out the software on their own and that too to a level that they can make the decision?" Liladhar said.

"In that case, why do CRM companies provide trials?" Shankar raised a genuine doubt.

"That is, in fact, their way of lead generation. They want to know who is looking for a CRM. It's for them, not for us," Liladhar clarified.

"Oh, Ok. I never realized that. But it sounds very logical, once you explained this now." Jagdeep seemed to be surprised.

"Also, A trial is for those who are already familiar with the concept and the tools for that purpose. So it's good for an expert. Definitely not useful for first time CRM buyers," Liladhar explained.

"You mean, it's like, If I don't know cycling, then how can I take a trial ride in a cycle store. I get it, now," Anubhav exclaimed.

"In that case, how do you suggest we make a buying decision?" Irshad asked, who had been listening to all this till now.

"Prepare a list and get a Guided Tour of the CRM Platform." Liladhar said, "Let me explain."

 CRM trial does not help the buyer.

Because a trial helps the vendor and not the buyer, CRM companies give trial software to get a list of people interested in buying CRM. It is not for helping the customer buy, but for the seller to get more leads.

---

3. Why are Guided Tours of CRM more beneficial?

Everyone in the room was listening intently. You could hear a pin drop. All of them wanted to know what the alternative to having a trial of CRM was.

"First, understand your process, write it down on a piece of paper. You don't need ISO-certified documentation for it. Just write it down." Liladhar continued.

"Then write down your requirements and expectations from the CRM. Don't worry about whether it is possible or not. Just jot down your entire wishlist." Liladhar said.

"But who should create that?" Shankar Narayan asked.

"Of course, this is not one person's job. You cannot google CRM requirement document and copy-paste it as your own." Liladhar said.

"Yes, I agree with Liladhar. I think the Sales Team or Service Team has to finalize the requirements document." Anubhav clarified.

"Instead of writing down the features required in CRM, write down what problems you want to solve. You focus on the problems so that the vendor can focus on solving them," Liladhar explained.

"Otherwise, both the parties get lost in the jungle of features, and nothing gets solved. We have experienced it," Shankar said. Now he realized what had gone wrong previously.

"Exactly! Always focus on solving the problem, not on features. Most of the rookie sellers will try to get you entangled in the components of CRM." Liladhar warned them.

"I agree with you, Liladhar. In both of our previous experiences, we had many discussions about the features. However, very few about our challenges," Anubhav added.

"Yes, Anubhav, I agree. Also, we did compare more than five CRM platforms before finalizing our current vendor. But something went wrong there," Shankar said.

"Comparison charts are generally useless." Liladhar exploded one more bomb.

"Explain, please," Jagdeep said. Almost everybody had expected Jagdeep to say this line.

 Get a Guided Tour instead of Self trial.

Instead of trying software on your own, ask for a guided tour. Create a list of your pain points and challenges, and then ask the vendor to show you how the CRM tool can solve your problem. Don't focus on the features; focus on the solutions.

4. Why are comparison charts useless?

"First of all, comparison charts are always biased. The vendor who prepares the charts will always create a comparison that favors them." Liladhar said.

"Yes, that sounds very obvious. But then is it a regular market practice to ask for a comparison chart before buying any product?" Shankar asked.

"You can compare something that you know. Suppose you already have good knowledge of Mobile phones. In that case, you can use comparison charts to compare them," Liladhar said.

"Comparison charts are for experts and not for the first time buyers. They are actually meant to confuse the buyer," Liladhar said.

"This means the trials taken by Sugandha and the comparison charts created are almost useless," Irshad said, with very natural frustration.

"Unfortunately, yes," Jagdeep replied.

"No," Anubhav said with a wicked smile.

Everybody thought that Anubhav had some idea to counter these arguments.

"In fact, it is fortunate that we are not going by trials and comparison charts. Otherwise, we all would have faced the same challenges that we have already faced twice," Anubhav clarified.

"Also, there is one more problem with the comparison charts. You see, if we create a comparison chart between a 2,00,000 Rs car (say a Tata Nano) and 5,50,00,000 Rs. Car (say a high-end Mercedes), 98.8% of the features would look similar," Liladhar explained.

"But they both are very different," Irshad said with surprise.

"That is because you already know a lot about cars. You see, that's why comparison charts make sense for experts only," Liladhar said.

"In a nutshell, comparison charts are biased and misleading, especially for non-experts," Jagdeep tried to summarise the entire topic.

"Now, you have explained to us that our methods were wrong. We are yet to get the best way to finalize the CRM." Irshad was now becoming impatient to know the final solution to all their confusing questions.

"Yes, Liladhar, how do we finalize the CRM with maximum confidence of success?" Anubhav asked.

"As we discussed, first, you create a list of problems that you want to solve. Then you get a guided tour or demo of the solutions from your vendors," Liladhar said.

"Is that all? What about if the demo is excellent, but the after-sales service is pathetic. How can we be sure that the vendor will help us in making CRM a success."

 Comparison charts are for experts.

If you are a first-time CRM buyer, don't trust comparison charts. They are biased. They don't reveal the real story. They will have lots of useless jargon.

---

5. Talk to some users of your CRM Vendors

"No, the first two steps only help you to shortlist the vendors. But for the final decision, you should talk to a few of their customers," Liladhar said.

"We had tried it. But many vendors don't have a policy of giving the customer reference." Jagdeep said.

"Simple, don't buy from them," Liladhar said.

"Is that all?" Irshad questioned.

"Yes, Just think of it. If CRM vendors have enough satisfied customers, why not flaunt that? Is it because they don't have enough satisfied customers? Are they afraid that someone will steal their customers?", Liladhar asked.

"Hmm. I see the point." Anubhav said.

"But isn't that time-consuming?" Irshad asked.

"Don't tell me that. You will spend or waste much more time in negotiations. Tell me yes or no?" Liladhar asked.

"Yes. The last time, our Finance team spent four months in the negotiations," Shankar remembered.

"Ok, So we need to call customers of CRM vendors and ask them, how is the after-sales support?" Jagdeep asked.

"No!" Liladhar.

"Then, what else do we need to ask?" Jagdeep was more than curious. "Come on, Liladhar, don't create suspense."

"After-sales support is the wrong criteria for solutions like CRM. Because generally, after-sales support is reactive. But in the case of CRM, we need proactive help. Help for implementing the change in our organization," Liladhar explained.

"Now, to answer your question, you need to ask three things," Liladhar said.

"The first question is: What kind of teething problems did they face and how did they overcome them? Here focus on overall change management and not just configuration of CRM," Liladhar said.

"What will that reveal?" Anubhav asked.

"It will tell you the possible challenges that you might also face. Also, you can learn from the mistakes of others by avoiding them," Liladhar said.

"The second question is: How did the CRM vendor help their clients in overcoming those challenges," Liladhar said.

Liladhar continued, "The answers to this question will reveal whether the CRM vendor understands the real problem or not."

"And what is the real problem?" Irshad asked.

"See, you are actually adopting two new things at a time—a new way of working and new technology. The problem is 80:20. 80% of the challenge is the new way of working."

"But isn't that our problem. Why will the CRM vendor support us?" Shankar.

"That's a fair question. The change management and HR-related problems you have to solve on your own. But you will need support from your CRM vendor. Don't worry; we will discuss this in detail when you implement CRM, later," Liladhar said.

"The third point to discuss is how they are using CRM right now. Get some live experience from their users," Liladhar said.

"Should we ask those customers to show us their CRM? But will they show us their CRM and data? Why?" Anubhav asked

"No. You don't have to see the data. Just talk to people. One caution, however. Talk to more than one person in that company," Liladhar said.

Jagdeep looked like he had almost figured out the solution to finally buying the CRM in the best way. But he had a small doubt.

"But, how can we decide by talking to only one client of the CRM vendor?" Jagdeep asked

"No, you have to talk to at least three clients from each vendor," Liladhar said.

Irshad saw one more benefit of talking to the clients. "I think talking to the clients of a CRM vendor is the best option for small companies," Irshad said.

Irshad continued, "See, large companies have enough resources to spend in analyzing the product and the team. But this idea of talking to the actual customers and users is the best and most efficient way of deciding a vendor."

"All right. So, I think we are all set to finalize the CRM vendors and close the deal. Let us have lunch and then depart," Liladhar said.

"Yes, Liladhar, the lunch is all ready; let us move to the lunch-room."

"But I think we should come back after lunch. I have a question". Irshad said.

"Ok, let us come back after lunch; we will discuss that over a coffee. Does that sound fair?" Liladhar asked

---

 Get Customer references and talk to them.

Talk to at least three customers of your CRM vendors to find out their experience. It is much more revealing than anything else. It might look time-consuming, but invest that time. Anyways, you will waste too much time on negotiations, instead invest it in customer reference.

---

6. Onsite or Cloud?

After a good *Rajdhani* Lunch, they gathered back at the conference room to discuss a few final doubts. *Rajdhani* is a famous *Thali* restaurant in Mumbai which serves its world-famous Gujarati meal.

"Yes, Irshad. Please shoot," Liladhar welcomed the final questions.

"Should we go for a cloud or onsite software?" Irshad asked.

"Actually, that is not the real question. To reach the real questions, I have to ask you - how does it matter?" Liladhar said.

"It matters a lot. Because if it is onsite, then we can have a one-time cost rather than a recurring subscription," Irshad countered.

"Also, our data will be safe if it is onsite," Shankar added.

"Ok, so there are two basic perspectives here: a one-time cost or a recurring payment and the data security," Liladhar explained.

"First, let us discuss data privacy and cloud," Liladhar continued.

"Yes, that is important because our customer data and sales information are in the CRM tool. If the data gets compromised, then we are doomed." Jagdeep added.

"100 years ago," Liladhar started with a perfect storytelling style. "Nobody kept money in banks, and everybody wanted to keep their money and wealth buried in their homes. Right?"

"Yes, but what it has to do with our discussion," Irshad asked.

"Question is why nobody trusted the bank, and what has changed now?" Liladhar asked, almost ignoring Irshad's question.

"Now, nobody wants to keep the money at home. Banks are obviously safer than our homes," Jagdeep replied.

"Why do we consider that the banks are safer now?" Liladhar asked.

"Obviously, they have better and costly security systems. They also have proper processes and mechanisms to keep things safe," Irshad replied.

"The same is the case with the Data. Data is much more secure in a data center as compared to our own offices. We cannot afford to have high-end security systems, firewalls in our office," Liladhar said.

"Yes, that is Ok; our data is safe from the outside world. But how do we make sure that our information is secure from the CRM vendor?" Irshad asked.

"That is the reason we have to discuss with the customers of CRM Vendor. They will be able to share their experience with us," Liladhar clarified.

"Wonderful idea!" Anubhav was all excited about this idea.

"Also, there are a few more reasons why we should have a CRM in the Cloud," Liladhar said.

Jagdeep said, "Explain, please."

"A CRM tool is a complex piece of software. It requires a lot of third-party API access. Further, it has to be on a very high-performance platform to enable mobile access," Liladhar said.

Shankar chipped in, "You are right Liladhar, most of the people think that CRM can run out of their old existing server lying idle in their office."

"Why not?" Irshad asked with ignorance.

"You will require multiple high-end servers for Application, Database, and high-availability. Plus, we need sophisticated security and networking framework," Shankar added. He had got a chance to flaunt his technological prowess.

"I agree with Shankar. Hosting an entire CRM onsite on your premises is a very costly affair. This is not advisable for small businesses," Liladhar said.

"Bhai, you have answered Shankar's question. What about my query? Should we go for a one-time cost or subscription model?" Irshad was becoming impatient.

"Subscription is better for both sides, especially for the customers," Liladhar said.

Jagdeep said, "Explain, please."

"What would happen if you paid a hefty price for software, only to realize after six months that it is not suitable for you?"Liladhar said. "Isn't it better to pay-as-you-go so that if you don't like the software or the service, you can leave the vendor? that too, without any substantial loss."

"Yes, that is right, but then this way, my expenses would go on increasing as my team grows." Irshad agreed.

"In modern times, we cannot think that way. We have to come out of that old CAPEX model of thinking," Liladhar said.

> **Modern CRM is not possible without Cloud and Mobile.**
>
> **Don't even think of having an onsite or in-house CRM if you have anything less than 500 users. The cost of infrastructure and maintenance will kill you. Come out of the old school CAPEX mindset.**

"What things would increase with an increase in your team size? Your salaries, office rent, electricity, expenditure on IT infra, and many more things," Liladhar explained. "Similarly, we should now consider the software productivity tools as a part of the CTC of an employee. These costs are not increasing in isolation."

Anubhav said, "Yes, I agree. We have to come out of that old mindset. I feel Subscription-based cloud CRM is the best option to go ahead."

"We also have to consider from the vendor's perspective when we negotiate the price," Liladhar said.

"Let me give you my experience. We had one software tool, which initially we used to sell for ten lacs (1 million) Rs." Liladhar started the narration of his story.

"Then our sales team observed that few of our clients found it out of their budget to invest Rs. 10 lacs as the initial cost. We should divide the cost as per-year payment," Liladhar said.

Everybody was listening eagerly, as they were expecting an unexpected twist in the story.

"Then, five years back, we made it on a subscription basis with two lacs per year. But then new problems started to appear," Liladhar said.

"What went wrong?" Irshad asked.

"Now, some of our clients who had come from a one-time cost mindset came up with another request. Now they had a problem with the same subscription amount every year," Liladhar explained.

He continued, "They wanted that the subsequent year subscription should be significantly less. In fact, it should be nominal."

"So, whatever way the vendor will keep the price, people will have objections," Liladhar concluded.

"Yes, but as a customer, we do have the right to negotiate." Jagdeep was surprised as Liladhar was speaking from the vendor's side and not their side.

"Of course, we have the right to negotiate, but let us also consider that if the vendor does not get enough money, how will they provide good service? Vendors have to remain profitable to provide us with good service," Liladhar argued.

"I think now that all the queries are answered, you can finalize with your CRM vendors and begin the journey. Now it is the right time," Liladhar said.

"Yes," Irshad said. "I also remember one famous dialogue of Bachchan from Trishul."

"Which one," everybody asked Irshad.

"सही बात को सही वक्त पे किया जाए तो उसका मज़ा ही कुछ और होता है" Irshad.

Since Shankar did not understand Hindi properly, Irshad translated to English for him, "If you do the right things at the right time, it has a different benefit."

Useful Info: Best process for buying CRM

1. Create a list of challenges you are facing or problems that you want to solve.

2. Write down processes that you want to manage with CRM.

3. Ask CRM vendors to give a guided tour of their products and show you how their software can solve your problems.

4. Ask for a list of at least three customers from every shortlisted CRM vendor.

5. Always choose a vendor who has written the CRM Implementation process, which their salesperson can explain adequately.

6. Talk to those customers and discuss the following points:

    a. What challenges they faced while implementing CRM, and how did they handle them.

    b. How did the CRM vendor help in resolving those challenges?

    c. Ask them how they are using their CRM currently and how satisfied they are with their usage.

7. Don't over negotiate. Since you don't know what they will deliver, CRM vendors may cut down the deliverables without your knowledge.

Chapter 3

Implementing CRM

तुम लोग मुझे वहाँ ढूँढ रहे थे और मैं तुम्हारा यहाँ इंतज़ार कर रहा हूँ

– Vijay (Amitabh Bachchan) in Deewar movie.

Now that all the friends understood CRM's advantages and how it will be beneficial for them, they quickly went about finalizing a CRM for their respective businesses. They were now eagerly working on the implementation of the software.

This time they were meeting after a whole month and not fifteen days. This time again, it was at Anubhav's office.

Liladhar had arrived in Mumbai a day before for his fortnightly Ayurved classes. He and Irshad were first to reach for the meeting.

As they were sipping hot masala tea, Jagdeep arrived. Anubhav had not yet reached his office. As usual, he was late. But Shankar had joined the meeting.

This time, Jagdeep's wife, Jaspreet, also joined him for the meeting.

"So, how did your CRM purchase go?" Liladhar asked.

"As planned," Jagdeep said. "Flawless."

After independently evaluating multiple service providers, they narrowed down to a single vendor. Eventually, they agreed to buy from the same vendor.

"Today afternoon, I have invited a Senior CRM Delivery head for our meeting here," Jagdeep said.

"Super," Liladhar replied.

Just then, through the spotless glass walls of the conference room, they saw many of the staff members standing up in respect to greet someone. It was apparent, Anubhav had arrived.

" My Apologies, Gentlemen, for being late." Anubhav offered a formal, corporate apology. "Aha, we are privileged to have a lady amongst us as well. How are you, Jaspreet?" he added.

Once everybody had settled down, Liladhar kicked off the discussion. "So, how is your CRM going now?

"We are making all the configurations," Shankar was quick to reply. "While CRM vendors are customizing the software to match our business requirements."

"They have an extremely user-friendly & easy-to-modify admin module, where we can modify the complete CRM system. " That's great! And what about others?" Liladhar asked, looking around.

" I agree about the ease of usability; though we don't have much customization to do, we are just making some field-level modifications based on the recommendation by members of our sales team," Irshad said.

"Jaspreet is coordinating with the CRM Vendor for the same. We should be up and running in about ten days," Jagdeep added.

"That's great. So have you all identified a person in your company who will take on the role of CRM Admin" Liladhar asked?

"What is a CRM Admin, and why do we need one? Do we hire a new person for this?" Jaspreet was nervous about this new revelation as it might add extra cost.

1. Roles, responsibilities, and qualities of CRM Admin

"Please understand, you and your CRM Solution provider will have to communicate and coordinate at multiple levels and many times. It will be easier if you have a single point of contact and communication channel between both the teams," Liladhar explained.

"The CRM Admin is a designated person from within your team, who will communicate with the CRM vendor company. The Admin ensures the success of CRM," Liladhar said as he further explained the benefits.

"In our case, Shankar is the CRM Admin, as he is the one who looks after all the technology deployments in our company," Anubhav replied.

"But in our company, we don't have a CTO. Do we need one?" Jaspreet said, getting more nervous.

"We don't have a CTO, either, Liladhar. You did not mention this before that we would need to hire a dedicated person for the CRM software," Irshad said.

"No, the CRM Admin is not a technical role. It is a managerial role," Liladhar explained. "BTW, you should never hire a new person for the role of a CRM Admin."

"It's not about configuration, but more about making the CRM successful, by proper adoption and utilization and making sure that people use the system to its fullest potential," Liladhar continued.

"What are the exact responsibilities of the CRM Admin?" Irshad asked curiously.

"Five. There are five fundamental roles of a CRM Admin.

1. Planning
2. Setting the process,
3. Training

4. Monitoring

5. Coaching.

Let us discuss one by one," Liladhar explained.

Planning:

"Depending on the organizational goals, the CRM Admin has to decide the expected results from the CRM. These goals are to be discussed with the Internal team members," Liladhar said.

"Are these similar to what we had shared with our solution providers?" Irshad asked.

Liladhar continued, "Yes, but in a more elaborate and detailed way. What you shared with CRM vendors were just pains and challenges. But for the internal team, you will need detailed benchmarks, goals to be achieved."

Setting processes:

"The second responsibility of the CRM admin is to set the processes which are to be managed by the CRM platform." Liladhar began the explanation.

"Is this same as the requirement document that was created with the CRM solution provider team?" Jaspreet asked.

"CRM, actually, captures only 10-40% of your entire process. Let me give you an example of our sales team," Liladhar continued.

"We sat with our sales team and then created a sales process for *Jarvis*, our low-cost personal Assistant product. Just a simple bullet list," Liladhar said.

"it was 78 lines on all the steps the salesperson had to do. All the questions and actions are covered. Out of 78 steps, how many steps do you think were covered by CRM?" Liladhar asked.

"Liladhar, you made a mistake. You already gave us the answer before giving the question. The steps in CRM must be between 7 to 30, between 10 to 40%." Irshad said with a mischievous smile.

"But then creating this document will take much time," Jaspreet said, as she was not aware of the discussion in the last meeting.

"No, Jaspreet, we don't need to have ISO-style documentation. Just sit with your sales team and list down the points. That's it. Am I right, Liladhar?" Irshad asked Liladhar.

"Absolutely right," Liladhar added. "Don't think of creating perfect documentation. Remember one thing - सोच गहरी हो जाए तो फ़ैसले कमज़ोर हो जाते है." (Meaning: Too much thinking dilutes your decisions). Done is better than perfect," Liladhar added.

"Also, we already have the Sales process set; why do we need to create the process again for the CRM tool?" Irshad asked.

"It would be good if you consider reviewing the process again. Because the tool to manage the process is going to change." Liladhar said.

Jagdeep said, "Explain, please."

"Ok, which tool have you been using to communicate and coordinate with your sales team?" Liladhar asked all of them.

"We have been using WhatsApp for day-to-day communication. Our sales team also submits a Sales report every Saturday." Jaspreet said, and Jagdeep nodded.

Irshad said that his team had a similar process.

Shankar and Anubhav looked at each other. "Well, on paper, we have had CRM to coordinate and track the sales team. But in the actual process, we use WhatsApp and Excel," Shankar said.

"Ok, We have to understand that *your existing processes are designed based on and around these tools. But when your tool changes, you can optimize your process to take maximum advantage of the tool*," Liladhar added.

"Does it really matter? I am still not clear about its importance," Irshad asked.

"Take the analogy of you cutting iron sheets with hand tools. What would the process be?" Liladhar asked.

Before anyone could reply, he said further, "Now, if you have a CNC cutting machine, what would the process be?"

"Yes, I see there will be a huge difference in the process," Irshad said.

"Now, Imagine what would happen if you follow the same process even after deploying a CNC machine," Liladhar challenged them.

"Obviously, we would not be using the new tool to its fullest," Jagdeep added.

"In the case of the CRM tool, most companies make this same mistake. They want to use the new CRM the way they used old tools," Liladhar said.

"For example, when you use a generic tool, you have to do much exercise for monitoring and tracking what's happening. But when you use a CRM tool, you can focus on more important matters," Liladhar added.

 Try redesigning your processes around the new CRM.

You designed your old Sales process as per the limitations of the tools you were using. Now that you have a much better and sophisticated CRM Tool, it's better to consider redesigning the process to take maximum benefit.

Training:

"The CRM Admin is responsible for the Training of the team," Liladhar said.

"But the CRM training has to be provided by the solution provider. Right?" Shankar asked.

"Yes, that is right. But the CRM vendor will provide training for the software. Who will provide training for the process?" Liladhar asked.

"Also, your process will change somewhat because of the new CRM platform. Your processes can become much more efficient." Liladhar added.

"Hmmm, I get it," Shankar nodded.

"Even though the CRM vendor will give the training for the CRM tool, the CRM Admin has to make sure that everyone gets that training seriously," Liladhar said.

Jaspreet asked, "What happens when a new person joins the team? Does the CRM vendor provide training for them as well?"

"Yes, we have already discussed this with our Vendor. They have promised us to do the onboarding every time a new person joins our company," Jagdeep replied.

"Generally, all the vendors provide onboarding services for new employees. But it is better to confirm this in advance. Otherwise, you might end up spending lots of training costs," Anubhav added.

"Yes, some of the MNC vendors have charges for everything. In that case, training for new employees can be very costly," Irshad said.

 Process training is different from CRM Training.

The sales process is much more elaborate and detailed than merely using a CRM tool. The CRM Vendor will provide training for CRM software. But you have to give the Sales Process training to your team.

Monitoring:

Liladhar continued, "The CRM Admin also needs to monitor whether the users are using the system properly or not?"

"Yes, I agree," Shankar added, "In all our previous experiences, we failed badly because our users did not use the system to its fullest."

"Yes, this is the fundamental reason why you should not have a new person as the CRM Admin. Your team members, especially senior team members, would not listen to the new person." Liladhar added.

Coaching:

"Liladhar, why do you mention training and coaching as two different roles of CRM Admin?" Jaspreet asked.

Jagdeep was happy because his wife, Jaspreet, took a keen interest in the CRM topic and this discussion. He wanted her to take up the role of the CRM Admin.

But, there was a question in his mind, "Before you answer Jaspreet's question. I have a question. Can we have more than one CRM Admin?"

"Yes, why not. But the primary responsibility should be with one person only. Otherwise, no one will do it. **Nobody does work assigned to anybody**," Liladhar clarified.

"Now, let me answer Jaspreet's question. The difference between training and coaching," Liladhar said. "If we search Google, we get the technical difference between the two terms."

"In a nutshell, training is more of transfer of knowledge, and coaching is more related to enhancing the person's skill," Liladhar said.

"Let us look at it like this. First, we provide training for Process and CRM. Then the CRM Admin will monitor whether everybody is using the CRM tool properly or not. Of course, there would be some gaps."

"Now, you need to coach your team for those particular gaps only. Hence the word coaching," Liladhar explained.

Anubhav added to this, "Also, ***monitoring and coaching will be a continuous process***, isn't it?"

"Yes," Liladhar confirmed.

 Five responsibilities of The CRM Admin.

The CRM Admin is a designated person from your company. The responsibilities of the Admin are Planning, Setting Process, Training, Monitoring, and Coaching. The Admin is responsible for the success of the CRM tool in the company.

Who will be the right person?

"Liladhar, as you said, that the IT head or CTO is not the right person for the CRM Admin, then whom do you suggest should be the CRM Admin?" Anubhav asked.

"Yes, because the roles and responsibilities that you mentioned for the CRM admin are very demanding. We don't have anyone of that stature in our team," Irshad said.

"You need to think again, buddy. Your team already has that kind of people," Liladhar told Irshad. "However, let us try to generalize the whole idea so that it will apply to all of you."

"To play the CRM Admin role, you need someone who has a leadership position, so that the Admin knows what the goals of the organization are," Liladhar said.

"Further, the CRM Admin needs to have the proper ***authority to create and modify the processes,***" Liladhar continued.

"Which means that we cannot assign this task to any new person," Irshad said.

"Bhai, don't you remember, नए धंधे में पुराना आदमी चाहिए, पुराने धंधे में नया आदमी चलेगा (you need senior person for the new job)!" Jagdeep teased irshad.

"Also, there is one more reason why you need someone from the leadership position," Liladhar said.

"Irshad, suppose you assign the CRM Admin role to a new person. You said that you have very senior people in your Sales team working with you for more than five years. Do you think they will listen to that new joiner?" Liladhar asked.

"Obviously not. Senior team members never take new team members seriously." Anubhav shared his experience (अनुभव)

Irshad still had an objection to this idea. "In that case, If I become the CRM Admin for my company, it's a problem. I am not very good with technology."

"Irshad, In our entire discussion of the roles and responsibilities of CRM Admin, did you see the role of technology anywhere? No." Liladhar explained.

◎ Who should be CRM Admin?

A CRM Admin should be someone from the leadership team, who has a deep understanding of Business, its goals. He or she has the authority to change the process as required. Finally, a CRM Admin should be someone to whom the entire team will listen and obey.

"But then, the CRM Admin also needs to configure the CRM tool. I mean the fields and module-level changes and create reports."

"Aha, I was expecting this question. But I am surprised why it came so late," Liladhar smiled.

Should the Admin configure the CRM tool?

"This is the mistake many people make. Especially those who have a technical background," Liladhar said.

"Did you know that Non-IT companies adopt CRM five times faster than IT Companies?" Liladhar asked Shankar and Anubhav.

"Come on, Lila, how can that be true? In fact, IT companies or people with a good IT background should be able to implement CRM faster," Anubhav said.

"Logically, yes. But the data says otherwise. Surprisingly, there is a valid reason for the extra time required," Liladhar smiled while resisting to reveal the secret.

"Explain. Please." Jagdeep said.

"Firstly, Non-technical people see technology as a force multiplier for their business. They are least interested to know how it works. They want to get the benefits. That too, ASAP." Liladhar explained. "Whereas Technical people think that they know everything," Liladhar continued. "So, they try to do it themselves. In that process, they generally mess up things."

"See, with all the due respect to all the technical people and CTOs of the world. But, when you configure the CRM, you will be doing it for the first or second time." Liladhar said.

"But, the CRM Vendor and their team have the experience of doing it hundreds of times. They have experience with many business models. Whereas you have the experience only of your business process." Liladhar said.

"Hmm, there is a point in your idea," Shankar said.

Anubhav added, "I think we should focus more on our business and let the CRM vendor configure the CRM."

"There is one more point which you can take care of here. Instead of treating your CRM vendor as a Chemist (or compounder), you better treat them as a Doctor." Liladhar

Jaspreet got the hint, "So you mean rather than telling the Vendor what to configure and how to configure, we should focus on telling them our problems. So that they can provide us the best possible solution."

"Exactly, see, you don't go to the Doctor and tell them to give you that red syrup or yellow pill. You tell them what troubling you is. You let them diagnose the problem and suggest the solution," Liladhar said.

"Now, I understand why IT companies take more time in implementing the CRM. They think they are helping, but actually, they are becoming an obstacle to the implementation process." Anubhav added. "Maybe we did the same thing in our previous experience."

"So, we need to get our teams to start using the CRM ASAP," Anubhav added. "Once I start getting reports from the CRM, my role will begin."

"I differ here a little, Anubhav," Liladhar said. "But before we discuss that, I think we should have one round of Masala Tea for all of us."

 IT companies take longer to implement CRM.

IT Companies take 3-5 times longer than non-IT companies to implement CRM. Maybe IT Company's knowledge of technology causes this. In contrast, Non-IT companies listen to the advice of CRM Vendors and get success faster. They see technology as a force multiplier, whereas IT companies see technology as something they trade daily.

2. What is the role of Bosses and Team Leaders in CRM Implementation?

"Get Involved," Liladhar said. "Bosses and team leaders should get involved in the CRM implementation process."

"By Team leaders, I mean Sales Managers and Senior sales team members."

"Maybe that was the problem with our last two CRM implementation experiences," Shankar said.

"Senior team was waiting for things to get implemented. Also, we found it difficult to convince our senior team to change. So we decided first to bring our Jr team into the discipline and then talk to the Senior team." Shankar said.

"Bosses need to do two basic things. The first is to make sure that they are using the CRM to key in their activities. Secondly, when they review the work of their team, always take CRM data and not any other data." Liladhar.

"But, we have a few reports which we have been using for a very long time. These reports are created in spreadsheets. I need my reports in that format only." Anubhav said.

"Yes, also, it would be difficult for seniors to learn the CRM. They don't have time." Shankar added.

"Tell me one thing. Do you keep a person for operating your mobile or WhatsApp? No. You use it yourself." Liladhar added, "When you get a new model or new software update, you learn the new version and then use it. Then why do you want someone to use CRM for you."

"We don't want them to learn the CRM or technology behind it. But you can at least learn enough to analyze the data. You don't need to create reports. But at least analyze the reports provided by CRM." Liladhar said.

"A study says that *the biggest obstacle to change in any organization is not from Juniors but seniors. Bosses are the biggest obstacle in adopting changes*."

"Anubhav Sir, we should evaluate the reporting structure in the new CRM. I am sure they also have some fantastic reports for analysis. Also, We will need your presence in training as well." Shankar told Anubhav.

"I strongly recommend that all the bosses and senior team members should attend all the training sessions for the process as well as CRM." Liladhar insisted with authority.

Jaspreet said, "Yes, Bosses need to adopt the change first." As if she was teasing her husband, Jagdeep.

"So the CRM admin is the person who will drive the CRM project in the company. Right?"

"Yes, and No," Liladhar said with a smile. "Yes, because it is the primary responsibility of that person. No, because it's teamwork and one person cannot make it successful."

"Can you suggest who should play the role of CRM Admin in our companies? It looks like we all have understood the theory, but we still need to have a practical demo." Irshad said.

"Sure," Liladhar said. "See, in your case, since the team is around 25, and you are three partners, One of you should take up this responsibility."

"Sounds logical; maybe I will take that up," Irshad said.

Jagdeep thought that Jaspreet, his wife, should be CRM Admin. "In our case, can Jaspreet play the role of CRM Admin?" He asked.

"No. In your case, since the Sales team is reporting to you. Actually, you should play the role of CRM Admin. However, you may take some help from Jaspreet. But, the final responsibility of the CRM success will be on your shoulders." Liladhar said.

"For Anubhav's team. The most appropriate person would be Shankar, but he will need very active support from Team leaders and Anubhav also." Liladhar said.

"So, you will have to call all the team leaders and hand over this responsibility to them collectively. Otherwise, it will fail." Liladhar said.

Shankar was pleased to know that other team leaders will also be responsible for CRM's success. "Yes, I agree. I think if we had involved our Team Leaders in previous CRM implementations, then it would not have failed."

"Yes, I will make sure that the entire top team participates in the CRM implementation," Anubhav added.

"One more thing, whenever there is a training session for Process or CRM Software, bosses and team leaders should always attend," Liladhar said.

"But the Seniors and team leaders have designed the process. Why do we need to attend the training." Anubhav asked.

"Think about it. We will discuss it later," Liladhar said.

3. How much data should we capture?

"How do we make sure that our team members input complete information in the CRM system," Jagdeep asked.

"Simple, make those fields compulsory. They cannot go ahead without making those entries," Shankar replied.

"Maybe, it's not that simple," Liladhar said. "Remember the concept of Policy, process, and culture, we discussed in our first meeting."

Shankar and Jaspreet looked surprised, as they were not part of that initial meeting. Then Anubhav explained to them with a "No-Parking" example.

"Making a lot of compulsory fields may actually either discourage people from using it, or they will input junk data," Liladhar said.

"How come?" Jagdeep asked.

"Let me give you an example of one of my friends from the IT Industry. They decided that they wanted complete data right from the inquiry stage. So they had eleven compulsory fields in their inquiry module." Liladhar said.

"The compulsory fields in the Inquiry module were, First name, Last name, Mobile Number, Email ID, Company name, Company address, Industry vertical, Number of employees, ERP brand used by the client and few others."

"So what's wrong with it." Shankar was amused because he thought that having better data would result in better CRM usage.

"Let us discuss what happens in the real-life scenario when you get an inquiry?" Liladhar started to tell the story. "What are the minimum details you generally have when you get an inquiry or a lead?"

Jagdeep shared his practical experience "Sometimes we get only the name and mobile number. Not even company name and email ID."

"Exactly. Now imagine what you would do if you have to make an entry in CRM with 11 compulsory fields. How would you enter that?" Liladhar asked.

"Either I would put all the dummy data in the CRM, or I would write down the details in my diary and enter in the CRM once I have all the details ready with me," Jagdeep said.

"hmm, this can be dangerous," Irshad said. "In an effort to get complete data, we may actually discourage our users from using CRM completely or putting in the wrong data.

"But then what do you suggest we should do to get correct and complete data?" Anubhav asked.

"Let me tell you what we do at our company. In every module, we have very minimum fields as compulsory. Generally, only one field is mandatory so that we don't get blank records." Liladhar told.

"But then your CRM data will be a mess?" Shankar asked.

"Nope, first of all, we believe that as far as CRM data is concerned, yes is more. There is no point in collecting the data which is never going to be used." Liladhar.

"Secondly, we have created a few reports which we call as DQM - Data Quality Management reports. Our CRM Admin talks about this in all our review meetings. She also gives examples to the users who are not using it correctly." Liladhar said.

"But, what difference does that make?" Shankar was still doubtful.

"You did not get it, Shankar. She tells the users to correct that data, then and there, in real-time. In that meeting itself," Liladhar explained.

"How many times can people repeat the same mistake when they know that they will have to correct it in the meeting, in front of all other members," Liladhar asked.

"But you have to do this permanently. All the time. This means that we will require a dedicated person for checking the data?" Jaspreet asked.

"No, Not at all. This activity is one time for the first few weeks. Till our team members get accustomed to making proper entries." Liladhar.

"My Yog Guru says that if you do something for 21 days, it becomes your habit. If you do something for 42 days, it becomes your nature." Liladhar.

"So we have to do this exercise for at least 21 days," Jagdeep said.

"Exactly," Anubhav added. "Maybe we had made the same mistake in our previous two efforts."

"Also, we have to take care of the Change-Appetite of our organization," Liladhar added. "Start with fewer fields and then slowly keep on adding fields to it."

"Let me give you an example of our company. In the initial days, for tickets, i.e., customer complaints, we had only three fields. Complaint type, customer name, and complaint status." Liladhar.

"But that means that we might be getting incomplete data. We will not be able to do a full analysis of it." Shankar asked.

"Don't worry about that. Having few fields with correct and complete data is better than having compulsory fields and not getting data. Remember, it's about getting your team habituated." Liladhar explained.

"Yes, I agree." We should start with fewer fields and then grow it as our team starts adopting the new system," Jaspreet added.

"But, what about the customization. Will the standard CRM fit our requirements? I mean, we have our own processes." Irshad asked.

"Yes and no," Liladhar said.

"Explain, Please," Jagdeep said.

4. Should customization be done in the initial phase or later?

"There are multiple factors to consider here. For Anubhav's team, they will, of course, need some customization. But, for both of you, I would suggest that you go ahead with the standard CRM." Liladhar said.

"Firstly, any CRM package that has been around for a few years has been built on best practices." Liladhar continued. "Why do we want to reinvent the wheel when it is already near perfect."

"hmm, it makes sense," Jaspreet said.

"Yes, consider that you are getting free consultancy for the best processes. In a way, it gives you a perfect excuse to bring about the long-awaited change in your organization." Liladhar explained.

"If at all you want to customize, think of changing the system after three or six months. By then, you will have a much more in-depth knowledge of the system's capabilities and also your requirements." Liladhar continued.

"Yes, I agree," Irshad added. "One of my friends got the CRM; they made some serious customizations to it for another seven months."

"After very rigorous testing, when they finally asked their team members to use it. They found that there were many flaws in the process." Irshad continued.

"Then, what did they do?" Shankar asked.

"You would be surprised. They told the Vendor to remove all the customization and reset the CRM to default settings." Irshad explained. "Now they are using it very efficiently. They also made some major integration with their ERP software."

"Yes, it's a bad idea for first-time CRM users to make customizations in the CRM. It generally fails." Liladhar added.

"What about us? You said that we would need some customization," Anubhav asked.

"Yes, since yours is a relatively large team, as compared to these two, you might have comparatively better designed and established processes. Rather than disturbing everything, you should stick to your processes and customize the CRM according to your requirements. But.. " Liladhar left the sentence incomplete.

"But. What? Anubhav asked.

"Just don't overdo it. Instead, explore the new concepts and new philosophy of the CRM product that you have just purchased. Remember, the new tool has new capabilities which you want to take advantage of." Liladhar said.

"Most of the time, people strip the CRM of all its features and best practices in the pursuit of customizing it," Liladhar added.

"Explain, Please." Jagdeep.

"You know that I had been cycling for a long time before I bought a motorcycle for my business. Also, I had a typical habit of stopping the cycle by pushing my legs to the ground, instead of braking." Liladhar

"What would happen if I asked my motorcycle vendor to customize the motorcycle so that I could stop it with my feet on the ground?" Liladhar said.

"Yes, it explains itself," Jagdeep said.

"A majority of the customization occurs because of our previous habits and tools. We need to evaluate the new possibilities with the new CRM tool. The chances are that we might have more efficient processes and better clarity." Liladhar added.

"But in our case, we cannot start using CRM before we get our quotation format customized. It's the most important thing for us." Jagdeep said.

 First-time buyers and CRM Customization.

If you are buying the CRM for the first time, don't do much customization. Instead, try to understand and adopt the best practices on which the CRM is built. Think of customization after three to six months. By then, you will have much more idea about the platform capability and also your requirements.

How vital is Quotation Format customization?

"Of course, your quotation format is important, as you and your customers have been used to it for a very long time now. But consider this, how important is a quotation in your sales process?"

"It is the most important part, as we get orders based on quotations only," Jagdeep said.

"Yes, that is right, it's the document that your customer receives based on which you get the order. But what else do you need to do after you get an inquiry? What other steps do you do in the Sales Process?" Liladhar asked.

"Well, lots of other things, of course, meeting, follow-up, the demo of our products, technical discussion, and negotiations," Jagdeep said.

"Exactly. Now, What is the most important and critical component of that sales process. The one thing without which entire sales process would be useless." Liladhar asked.

"Maybe Demo of our product," Shankar replied.

"No, in my opinion, Negotiations are the most important part," Jagdeep said.

"Think a little more. What is one thing, which if not done properly, would kill the entire Sales process." Liladhar asked again.

"Follow up. Yes, I think that follow up is the main backbone of the sales process. If timely and proper follow-up is not done, then we won't get a chance to give a demo or do negotiations." Irshad said with a eureka excitement.

"Exactly. You are on the dot. 78% of sales are lost due to lack of proper follow-up." Liladhar said. "So, now what would you focus more on? Follow-up or Quotation?"

"There is one more perspective on this. ***What percentage of a sales person's salary do you attribute to creating a quotation.***" Liladhar asked.

"I did not get the question, exactly," Shankar asked.

"Suppose you are paying 40,000 Rupees to a Salesperson per month. What portion of it is towards creating quotations. AND, how much is for the rest of the activities like Follow up, discussions, meetings, understanding requirements, customer qualification, and negotiation."

"Hmm, I get the idea. You are right; the quotation is not the most important part of a salesperson's role." Anubhav nodded.

"But our entire process revolves around the quotation," Jagdeep said.

"In that case, you should go for some quotation management solution. Why go for a full-fledged CRM. It will be a waste of money." Liladhar said. "Ok, where do you make Quotations?"

"We make quotations in Google Spreadsheets. It's very flexible, and it allows us to change everything as per our need for every customer," Jaspreet replied. Many times, she had to create and manage quotations as it involved complex costing calculations.

"In that case, there are minimal chances that you will be satisfied with the Quotation formatting and customization. Structured software like CRM can never provide flexibility like a spreadsheet," Liladhar said.

"How about continuing the quotation creation process in Excel and managing the rest of the sales process in CRM? You can always attach the PDF file or link of the spreadsheet in the CRM," Liladhar added.

🎯 **The sales process is more than sending a quotation.**

Even though the Quotation is the document based on which you get the orders, It is not the most critical part of your sales process. Your Sales team is doing many other activities, which are far more essential than quotation alone. Finally, if you think that quotation is the most crucial part of your sales process, get good quotation management software. Why invest in a complete CRM tool?

"In my company, we have been using CRM for years. But till today, we don't have to create a quotation in our CRM compulsorily. Everybody makes quotations according to their set formats in Spreadsheet or Document editor. But most important is the actual sales process, which is managed in the CRM.

Quotations and Proposals

"Yes, but in our case, our different solutions need a different quotation format. Hence we cannot go ahead without customization work," Shankar said. "Actually, for our projects, we need a very detailed quotation, which runs into several pages. I am wondering how it will fit in our CRM."

"First, we need to understand the difference between quotation and proposal. A quotation is generally a structured one-page document, which lists down the items, quantities, and pricing. In comparison, a proposal is something that runs into several pages. The proposal has many details about the company, about the product and actual solutions," Liladhar said.

"It's a good idea to use a CRM tool for quotations. But not for Proposals. Instead, you should continue what you are using for proposals," Liladhar added.

Anubhav said, "Yes, Shankar, I think Liladhar is right. We should ask our project team to create the quotations in the same tool. But we should get all the sales related information in the CRM."

"Yes, getting a clear picture of the sales process and salesperson's activities was the main agenda behind buying the CRM tool. We cannot allow quotation customization to override it," Jaspreet added.

"So, I hope that sorts out everything? Or do you have any other questions?" Liladhar asked.

"We are almost ready to start using the CRM once our existing data is imported in the CRM," Irshad added.

Quotations v/s Proposals.

If you are into high-end solutions or projects, you send proposals to your clients instead of quotations. Proposals are very different from quotes and very complicated too. It is a bad idea to even think of having proposals created in the CRM. You will just waste your time and get frustrated.

5. Don't wait for importing old data into the CRM tool

"Ok. where is your data currently stored?" Liladhar asked.

"Well, we have lots of customers and potential customers data. We have data in our Outlook, mobile, Tally software," Irshad replied. "Also, we have lots of excel files containing old data which was collected since our inception."

"We have similar data, and above that, we have some more marketing data which we had purchased from a data vendor from Delhi," Jagdeep added.

"What about those thousands of visiting cards that we collected since we started our business. We should put all that data also into the CRM. So that it can be organized and used properly." Jaspreet added to Jagdeep.

"Ok, so how much time will it take for you to bring all this data in one spreadsheet in one format, properly organized? How much time do you require to create correct, complete, and consistent data?" Liladhar asked.

"Well, I thought it could be imported to the CRM directly, as it is. CRM Vendor had told us that they could import data into CRM. It's easy," Irshad asked.

"Yes, of course, you can import data into CRM, but then that data has to be in a proper format. Clean of errors and duplication," Shankar said.

"In that case, it won't be possible to clean the data before importing. Can't we import all the data in the CRM and then clean it there." Jagdeep said. "I am sure CRM has a good deduplication and data cleaning tool."

"One question, Why do you need all that old data?" Liladhar asked.

"We will organize everything, and then one day, we will start some business with them. We want to use all that data and make some money out of it. You know data is the new gold," Jagdeep said.

"Data is new Oil and not gold," Jaspreet corrected.

"Whatever, but you all got the point. Right?" Jagdeep smiled.

"When are you planning to organize and process that data?" Liladhar asked.

"Not immediately, But sure one day," Irshad replied.

"In that case, I would suggest keeping the data in spreadsheets. Use some other tool to consolidate and organize the data. You don't need new storage space for your garbage," Liladhar suggested.

"What do you mean garbage?" Irshad asked.

"See, if you want to use the data, it has to be in some form of actionable Information. Incorrect, incomplete, and inconsistent data is not useful information, but it's a garbage collection. As of now, that garbage is in spreadsheets and other software. Why do you want to put all that garbage into CRM?" Liladhar asked.

"But what is the harm in putting all the data in the CRM," Anubhav argued.

"If you know that your CRM contains incorrect information, you will not trust it. If you don't trust it, then you will not be able to use it. The entire CRM project can fail because of this garbage data."

"If you want to use the data, first prepare a proper plan for it. First, organize and consolidate the data." Liladhar said.

"What tool should we use to organize the data?" Jaspreet asked.

"But, let me warn you, using openrefine is not easy. There is a steep learning curve. You will have to spend some time learning it." Liladhar added.

"I will study it and share my findings with you all," Shankar added.

"Does it mean that we have to forget our existing data?" Irshad asked.

"No. absolutely not. That is your prized collection, an asset that you have built over the years. You just make sure that you don't convert your CRM tool into a data garbage collection point." Liladhar said. "If you have old data, then first clean it and then import it as and when required."

"Ok, in that case, what do we import first? I mean before starting to use the CRM." Jaspreet asked.

"Import your current leads, tickets, current customers, etc. That is enough to get you started," Liladhar replied.

"Is that enough?" Jaspreet asked in surprise.

"Yes, of course, it is enough for you to get started. You will build the data as you go along. When you are ready with other data and respective processes for it, you clean the data and import it," Liladhar said.

Anubhav said, "Yes, I agree with Liladhar. Even in our previous CRM, we had tried to import all the old inquiries. As a result, all our sales reports were useless. Then we moved to Excel for reporting. Maybe that is the reason CRM never took off."

"Also, when we prepared the data for importing in the CRM for the first time, it took almost four months. So, till that time, our CRM implementation was on hold." Shankar confessed.

"Yes, I remember. At first, I was furious with the CRM vendor, but then I realized that it was not their problem. The delay was on our side," Anubhav admitted.

"Never delay your CRM implementation because of data import, especially when you are a first-time user. Just start using it. Importing your old data will only increase your work if not done properly," Liladhar added.

"Ok, it's decided then. We are going ahead and starting to use the CRM tool. Jagdeep, you take the training so that all our team members can start using the CRM," Jaspreet instructed her husband.

"Once again, I feel that you should think once again on doing so," Liladhar added.

 Before importing your existing data to CRM.

Don't make CRM a new place for your data garbage. Don't import data without cleaning and correcting it. Don't import data that you don't plan to use in the near future. Most importantly, don't postpone your CRM usage for Data import. Sometimes, many companies take months to prepare their data for imports.

"But before we discuss the Training part, let us first finish the lunch. I have ordered a special Italian lunch from the famous *Celini* restaurant," Anubhav interrupted him.

6. Is CRM Training required? For whom?

After the Italian lunch, they gathered again in the same lavish conference room. The conference room contained a few large paintings of famous people. Anubhav had a story for it. All these people were achievers: successful sports personalities, business leaders, and political leaders.

Anubhav said, " I feel that when you are in the conference room, you see these pictures, and they inspire you."

Liladhar said, " I must say that the conference room has positive vibes."

"Why do you want Jagdeep to take the training when the entire sales and service team use the CRM?" Liladhar asked.

"Why waste everybody's time in taking the training. Anyways, our users are very tech-savvy. They are already using WhatsApp, Facebook, Gmail, and other things. In fact, they use their mobile phones all the time. I don't think that they require training." Jaspreet said. "If they require it, Jagdeep can train them."

Irshad added, "I would first like to take the training, understand everything, and then provide the training to my team. So that I am clear about the functionalities before my team gets training for it."

"Tell me one thing. Do you often do training with your team? I mean, do you have a regular training culture?" Liladhar asked.

"Yes, we do have regular product training. Our suppliers send their technical team to train our technical staff and sales staff," Irshad said.

"No, I mean training for the process. Training on how to do something." Liladhar asked again.

"No, we have never had that kind of training. Actually, we never required one," Irshad said.

"But why are you asking? Is something wrong with this idea? I mean, everybody uses the train-the-trainer concept. It saves time and also many resources," Jagdeep said.

"Train-the-trainer does not work, especially in a small organization. Also, when we don't have a regular training culture, it fails completely," Liladhar said.

"Let us dig deeper. Suppose you took the training. How much of it do you think you will retain? And for how long?" Liladhar asked.

"Maybe 80-90%. How long, I am not sure," Jagdeep said.

"Ironically, research says that people forget 50% in one hour, 70% in one day, and 90% in one week," Liladhar said.

"Interesting," Irshad said.

"Which means that if you take the training, and then you give the same training to your team. There are chances that you will be able to transfer only 10-20% of what you learned." Liladhar said.

Jaspreet was surprised, "imagine how much they would remember," she said.

"Plus, the trainers with CRM vendors are trained for providing training," Liladhar added.

"Yes, that's ok, but even when we buy any technology for ourselves, only Shankar and his few team members take the training. For example, last month, we bought a comprehensive Security and firewall system. It was only Shankar's team who took the training. " Anubhav said.

"There is a fundamental difference between a firewall and a CRM. I agree that all your users benefit from the Firewall, but they are passive users of it. They don't need to know how it works. It's not their business. But CRM is different." Liladhar said.

"CRM is a software that is going to help you manage a business process. The Sales Process. You don't want me to tell you that in every organization, perhaps sales is the only most unorganized team of all." Liladhar continued.

"All your sales team members will have to thoroughly understand the Sales process and CRM software to take maximum advantage of the same," Liladhar added.

"Training is a must for every member of the team," Liladhar emphasized.

"But our senior team leaders don't have time to take the training," Shankar said. "They are too busy with their regular activities."

"We just discussed before lunch that all the bosses and team leaders need to attend the training along with the members. I think that is the best way to convey that you are very serious about the whole CRM thing." Liladhar said.

"In fact, we also have a similar problem. My two other partners and one senior salesperson do not like this idea of training at all in my organization. They do the work, but in their style." Irshad said.

"So, I think that first, we will start with the training of junior team members, let them adopt the CRM. Once the junior team members have started to use the CRM, then the seniors will not have a choice but to adopt the change." Irshad added.

"Does it mean that Juniors will drive change in your team?" Liladhar asked. "Also, it passes a message to Junior team members that if you become Senior, then you don't have to follow the rules."

"So, once they become Senior, they will also stop following the processes," Liladhar concluded.

"Hmm, I understand now. Maybe that is the reason why our sales team always struggles with any process. I will try to convince them." Irshad said.

"I strongly recommend that you discuss with both the partners and senior salesperson. They need to help you in driving the change." Liladhar added.

"Remember, CRM is about the change in your organization's working style. Don't look at it like any other software. It has to be managed like any other change is managed." Liladhar said.

⊙ **CRM Training Tip.**

CRM Training is different from your Process Training. First, give process training and then CRM training for your team. Insist on training each and every team member, even the most senior people in the company. Training has to be regular and compulsory.

Just then, Bhamini Trivedi, the Senior CRM success officer, arrived from the CRM vendor's team. She was here to discuss the implementation process and clear some pre-implementation doubts that these people had.

After a formal introduction with Bhamini, Irshad, Jagdeep, and Shankar explained to Bhamini what they had discussed with Liladhar. Bhamini was thrilled that Liladhar had made her work very easy by convincing many points to these people.

"Liladhar Sir, a big thank you to you for helping me in this. Your guidance to these people has made my job easy," Bhamini said.

"I should get a consultancy fee then. Liladhar said, "Just joking. I was just sharing my experience with my friends. I am glad that it is useful for them.""

"I am here to discuss the formal process of implementation. How we will coordinate the entire process with your teams." Bhamini said.

"I have a question before that." Jagdeep asked her, "Why do you have two modules to manage the sales cycle. Why don't you just call it an inquiry or a lead."

"Why do you have Leads and Opportunities? Or sometimes your team calls them inquiries and deals. It is very confusing." Jagdeep continued.

7. Should you use Leads, opportunities, or both?

"Sir, In fact, apart from Leads and opportunities, quotations are also used in the sales process," Bhamini clarified. "However, it is not compulsory for you to use all the modules. You should use modules according to your requirements."

"That's Ok; I understand the purpose of the quotations module, but why these two modules?" Jagdeep asked.

"Let us divide the Sales process into two parts, before qualification, and after qualification. Leads module is before the qualification process. Qualified leads become opportunities," Bhamini said.

"Ok. So, when a customer agrees to buy the product, we have to enter into a deals module?" Jagdeep asked.

"No. It's not like that," Bhamini explained, "Actually, the qualification process depends upon your organization. It varies from customer to customer."

"Let me try to explain," Liladhar interjected in the discussion. "There are more than one ways to look at this. Let us start with the simplest one."

Why is the Qualification process essential?

"When we receive any lead, there are chances that we don't have much information about potential customers. Hence we put that details in the leads module. Generally, the leads module will have much less information as compared to the opportunity module," Liladhar explained.

"Does it mean that once we get all the information about customer's requirements, we should enter details into the opportunity module?" Jagdeep asked, slightly impatiently. He was intrigued. Why did these CRM vendors make it complicated?

"Not exactly. It's the progress of the sales process. But the actual reason for having two modules, as Bhamini rightly said, is the qualification process," Liladhar said.

"The qualification process is where you determine whether or not the prospective customer is a good fit for your product. This can be based on various parameters," Liladhar continued. "There are various ways of qualification. Let me explain to you how I look at it."

"Ask two questions of yourself. Can I provide the customer what they are asking? And can the customer provide me what I am asking?" Liladhar explained. "If the answer to both the questions is yes, then the lead is qualified."

"But for that, we need to know a lot more about the customer's requirement, their budget, other competitors, the pricing offered by them, etc." Jagdeep was more confused now.

"Think again. Of course, you need to ask questions and collect the information. But it is not the final decision of the customer. It's your decision, whether you want to follow up this inquiry or not," Liladhar explained.

"It's much before that. It's when you decide that you want to take this ahead. Because obviously, entertaining each and every inquiry with everything you have does not make logic." Liladhar continued.

"Let me give you an example. You are dealing in gears, right? But you deal in particular types of gears only. You don't deal in every type of gear on the earth, correct?" Liladhar asked Jagdeep.

"Yes, we deal only in small-size gears," Jagdeep replied.

"So what would you do when you get an inquiry for a large size gear," Liladhar asked.

"We reject that inquiry," Jagdeep said. " We don't follow up with them. We tell them up front that we don't deal in those products."

"Exactly, that is the purpose of the inquiry module," Liladhar said.

"Consider the Leads module as a doorkeeper that you have on the door of your shop."

Shankar and Anubhav looked at each other because they have been doing it wrong in their previous CRM experience. Shankar said, "I think that was the problem with our system. Our sales team used to convert an opportunity, only when the customer had promised them a PO."

"As a result, your opportunity winning ratio is always 100%, which is never possible in real-world scenarios," Liladhar said.

"Hmm." Anubhav nodded as he went in flashback, thinking about the confusions they used to have in Sales review meetings.

"But in our case, sometimes we are not sure whether the customer will buy from us until we show them the product demo and understand their requirements in detail, which requires a lot of time. What should we do in that case?" Anubhav asked.

"Good point. Two questions. Do you do these two steps for each and every customer? And when do you decide whether the demo and requirement-meeting are required or not?" Liladhar reciprocated with another set of questions.

> **A properly designed lead Qualification process is a must.**
>
> **Qualified leads are to be converted to Opportunities. The lead qualification process is crucial for the efficient working of the Sales team. Otherwise, your sales cost might increase.**

"Obviously, no. By our experience, we know whether we should follow up or not. Also, we don't work on projects below 100 seats. So if the Inquiry is below 100 seats, we don't entertain," Anubhav said.

"See, you have answered your question," Liladhar smiled. He further added, "Once you decide that you want to follow up that inquiry, it becomes a deal."

"There is a hidden purpose of these two modules. It helps you to analyze your marketing efforts and sales efforts," Liladhar added.

"Wow, that is interesting. Please explain that," Jagdeep said curiously.

"Before that, I have one question. What should we do when we get an inquiry from our existing customers?" Irshad asked.

Inquiry from existing customers

"Generally, when you get an inquiry from your existing customers, there is no need to enter them into the Inquiry module. You can directly enter them as Opportunities. The reason is that you already know the client and also their requirement. Maybe, you can skip the qualification process," Liladhar explained.

"I want to ask a question. Not related to CRM, but related to Sales." Jaspreet said, looking at Jagdeep. She seemed a bit reluctant to ask the question.

"Please go ahead. I will definitely answer it, I mean, If I know the answer," Liladhar said.

How much time should you require for Lead qualification?

"For how long should we retain the inquiry in the leads module before converting it to an opportunity?" Jaspreet asked.

"Before I answer, I will request others to attempt this," Liladhar said.

"Maybe a few days, or a week," Shankar suggested. Jagdeep and Irshad.

"What do you think, Anubhav?" Liladhar asked.

"I think it should be a few hours or a couple of days. Because, now that it is clear that the leads module is only used for qualification, we have also understood what is qualification. It should not take us more time for qualification," Anubhav said.

"You are bang on, Anubhav," Liladhar said with appreciation.

Now, Anubhav had started getting interested in the discussion. He generally would not get involved in these things. He was usually interested in the results. But now, things had begun to change.

"If your team is taking more time to qualify means that they need proper training in the qualification process. Maybe, you need to define a proper qualification for the same," Liladhar said.

"You were going to tell some secret purpose of the lead and opportunity module," Jagdeep returned the discussion to its original flow.

"For that, we have to play a small game. Are you all ready for it?" Liladhar asked.

"Yes, of course. In fact, it would be better after lunch to do something exciting,' Jagdeep almost jumped from his seat.

Liladhar went to the whiteboard and created a chart as follows:

Stages	Team A	Team B
Inquiries created (or generated)	100	100
Leads qualified (or opportunities created)	80	20
Sales Closed.	10	10

"Now, I have a question for you?" Liladhar said, pointing at the whiteboard. "Both the teams are in the same industry, with a similar product. What conclusions would you draw from these numbers?"

Shankar was very quick to reply. "Effectively no difference, because both got 100 leads and made ten sales. So the end result is the same in both cases."

"No, Shankar. If there would have been no difference, then Liladhar would not have put up this question," Anubhav said. "I think team B is good at closing the deals."

"Ok, let us have some more observations," Liladhar said. "BTW, there is no single answer to this. There can be many observations. This exercise will expand your understanding of these two concepts and also about your sales process."

"But Anubhav, we can also say that Team B did a pathetic job at qualification. They might have disqualified many eligible inquiries. See, they only qualified 20 leads out of 100 that they had received," Jagdeep added.

"Let me help you with some more information. Let us put the teams responsible for these results, stagewise. So that you at least know whom to blame or praise.' Liladhar said. He walked up to the board and added one more column to the table.

Stages	Responsible for results	Team A	Team B
Inquiries created (or generated)	Marketing Team.	100	100
Leads qualified (or opportunities created)	Inside Sales Team.	80	20
Sales Closed.	Sales Team.	10	10

"Now, I have added the names of the teams responsible for the results," Liladhar said. "Marketing is responsible for generating leads. The inside sales team does the job of qualifying those leads."

"But in our case, we don't have an inside sales team," Jagdeep said.

"No problem. That does not matter. Someone in your team is doing that role. Even if you have a one-person sales and marketing team, these are the three roles that you will have to do." Liladhar continued. "Generate the leads, then qualify them, and then finally process them to the Sales."

"Now, it makes much more sense. I think that the Inside salespersons of Team B did not do a good job. They rejected most of the leads. Otherwise, their sales might have been much more," Anubhav came to a quick conclusion.

Irshad, who was quiet for some time, had a different opinion. He said, "But Anubhav, it can also be a case, that the marketing team of team B, generated very pathetic inquiries. These were non-relevant leads. Hence they got disqualified. In fact, they wasted the time of the Inside Sales team."

"Hmm, that is also the possibility," Anubhav replied. "But how do we know for sure where the problem is?"

"That is the beauty of this exercise. Now, you are using your assumptions. But in real life, you will have real data to do real analysis. You will be able to find out what is the exact problem with the Sales process," Liladhar clarified. He added, "But there are still many more observations possible from this table. Please go ahead, think it out."

"Is it also possible that the inside sales team of team A did a horrible job at qualification? This way, they wasted the time of the Sales team." Jagdeep raised his previous point again.

"Yes, it is 100% possible," Liladhar said.

"So, you see that this table brings out inefficiencies in the entire system. This can be a great way to control the cost of sales." Liladhar said. "For example, in this case, the team A might have spent much more than the other."

Reducing the cost of Sales by analyzing leads v/s Opportunities

"But the end result is the same. How can we say that?" Jagdeep asked.

Anubhav was intrigued the moment he heard the word "cost." He asked, "I also want to know how there is a difference in the cost involved between two teams."

"Generally, in B2B Sales, the process of actual sales is much longer and costlier It involves experienced salespeople. Many times even the technical team is required for doing POC, Demos, and Technical discussions," Liladhar said. He continued, "whereas the cost of sales in B2C industries is much lesser and the spend on marketing is much more important."

"What is POC?" Jaspreet asked.

"Proof of Concept. Many times, clients want to check the solution in their environment. Hence they ask you to set up the same. To check how it works in their environment. It is prevalent in the IT Industry," Shankar said.

"Thanks, Shankar. There is a cost to generate the lead. Then there is a nominal cost for qualifying the leads. But suppose the qualification is not done properly? In that case, the Sales team ends up following up with the wrong prospects, which creates inefficiency in the sales process. Thereby increasing the cost," Liladhar explained.

"Wow, That was really an interesting secret. I must say that in our previous experiences, we never looked at our CRM tool in such a way," Anubhav said with excitement.

Even Bhamini Trivedi, who was the CRM consultant from the CRM Vendor company, was surprised. She confessed that none of their customers were using their CRM tool for such an analysis. "This is even a learning for me, Sir," she said.

 The Secret use of Leads and Opportunities module.

An in-depth analysis of the Leads and opportunities module can tell you how efficiently the teams are performing. The marketing team (responsible for generating leads), the Inside sales team (accountable for lead conversion), and the Sales team (responsible for closing sales), can work most efficiently using these two modules.

"Bhamini, before we start the implementation discussion, we also need to discuss the security. I mean, we don't want everyone on our team to see everything. People should be able to see the information, on the need to know basis." Jaspreet said.

8. Designing best Rights and Permissions for CRM

"Yes, definitely, Sir. We have a detailed right, roles, and permissions management option in our CRM. In fact, that is combined with the team's configuration also. This makes it immensely flexible." Bhamini said. She continued, "You can decide who can see what, when, and how much."

Shankar added, "Yes. The last time we had a nightmare configuring security. It was one of the most complex tasks."

"Shankar, was it because the software did not allow it or some other problem?"

"Firstly, because the CRM configuration was complex. But later, the problem got escalated, since our team members could not use it effectively because of the permissions that we had set," Shankar said.

"You are right, Shankar. Many of our clients overdo the permissions part, because of which the CRM becomes almost unusable."

"Please, explain," Jagdeep said.

"Let me give you an example." Bhamini started the explanation. "Let us assume that we have not allowed access to company data to the users. Now, your support executives need to access company data since they have to visit the client place."

"In this case, either the users will start keeping the contact details in some other tool, or they will not do the work. They will give reasons that the information is not available in the CRM," Bhamini continued.

"In fact, there is one more problem. Some companies do not allow regular users to create and edit the master records," Bhamini said. "So if the phone number of some client has changed, the user cannot update that information in the CRM since they don't have permission to access those records."

"So, What has the learning been, Shankar?" Liladhar asked.

"We need to think practically before setting permissions. Also, since we discussed previously, we should avoid doing the changes on our own. Instead, explain the requirement to the CRM Vendors. Let them do the changes," Shankar said.

"We would be happy to help you with everything," Bhamini said. "Since our team will understand the implications of the changes, before making the changes. Your team will not get stuck."

"Although the CRM software allows very complex roles and permissions to be set. I suggest that Irshad and Jagdeep should go ahead with default settings in the initial days. Get your users accustomed to the entire system and then make necessary changes." Liladhar said.

"But, then will it expose our data to our users?" Jaspreet asked.

"Don't worry. It is only for the initial few weeks. Afterwards, you may change the settings. Otherwise, if there is any record that they are not able to access, they will blame the CRM tool," Liladhar said.

"But should we allow all the users to create master records? They could mess up all the data. Instead, I think we should allow only a few persons to make changes in the master record," Jaspreet said.

"This sounds good to hear. But it will create a bottleneck in the organization. You will end up having lots of excuses from people," Liladhar explained.

"Yes, we had experienced that. Not having proper rights is a big hindrance to user adoption." Anubhav added, "In fact, it is a better idea to check the data after they have entered, and periodically point out their mistakes."

"This way, the culture of correct data will develop," Liladhar added to Anubhav's lines. "For first-time users, it is better not to create a complex web of permissions. Just make sure that you don't allow your users to export all the data."

"Cool, sounds good to me. We will go with the default permissions. We will just restrict the export permission, as you mentioned," Jaspreet seemed to be convinced.

 Setting rights and permissions for the CRM.

You don't need a watertight security system while in the implementation stage. If you are a small team and first-time CRM buyer, don't do the security settings for the first three months.

"Bhamini, how long will it take for the implementation to complete?" Irshad asked.

9. The ideal CRM Implementation Process

"It's not a single line answer, sir," Bhamini said. "Rather than discussing the time, let us first understand the process. That will help both the sides to understand the entire process."

"BTW, you can start using a CRM tool in 60 minutes from now. All of your users can, " Bhamini added.

"In one hour? Are you kidding?" Irshad asked.

"No, Sir, I am not. I am serious. But before I explain to you how to start using the CRM now. First, let us discuss the entire process in our company," Bhamini replied.

"Yes, Please," Jagdeep said.

"We will start with helping your team to install the Mobile App. Then, we have one onboarding session, which is 20 minutes for each team member," Bhamini said.

"Direct Mobile App? Don't you have a web version of the App?" Irshad asked.

"We do. The web app is much more comprehensive, But it would be much easier to get the users started with the mobile app. Also, we have a Mobile-first philosophy even at the product development level," Bhamini said.

"Also, there are some features in the mobile app that you can start using even without having a detailed knowledge of how CRM works," Bhamini added.

"Which are those features, may I ask?" Jagdeep asked.

"Our mobile app allows you to log your calls, start using SMS, Email, and WhatsApp directly from the App. These functions are straightforward to learn and do not require much involvement of the user," Bhamini replied.

"Also, you start building your database from day one," Bhamini added.

"Meanwhile, we will request all of you to nominate one CRM-Admin from your teams, who will coordinate with our team," Bhamini said.

"Yes, we have had a very detailed discussion on the CRM Admin part. We have already decided that," Shankar said.

"So who is going to be the CRM Admin?" Bhamini asked.

"Jagdeep, Shankar, and Irshad from their respective companies," Liladhar said. "Jagdeep and Irshad are owners of their companies, so they are perfect for the role."

"Shankar will share that responsibility along with three other Sales Managers and one service head and one VP projects," Anubhav said.

"Wow, that is so perfect. I must say that Liladhar had guided you very well. I must thank him once again," Bhamini said.

"How do we coordinate the entire CRM implementation process?" Jaspreet asked.

"We will have a WhatsApp group. We put your entire team, our CRM Implementation team members, I will be there, as will one of our directors in the group," Bhamini assured.

"We will use this group for coordinating everything regarding the Implementation process and day-day progress on the same," Bhamini added.

"But why do you need an entire team in the WhatsApp group? That will create unnecessary chaos. The whole purpose will get defeated," Shankar said. "Everybody will write all their complaints there, and everything will get lost."

"That is the actual purpose, Sir. We want everybody to write their doubts and queries there immediately. As soon as they have a query, we want them to write it there," Bhamini said. "This, in fact, creates transparency and increases the user adoption right from the beginning."

Shankar said, "But previously, we had only one person communicate with the CRM vendor. All the team members used to share with me, and I spoke with the CRM vendor. All our team members are not experts in Software App. You will unnecessarily get flooded with unwanted queries."

"I think she is right," Liladhar said, "This way, no one will get a chance to give excuses. Regarding the queries, don't worry about that. Bhamini and her team can handle that."

"Also, why do you want to take responsibility for handling all the support related queries? Let the CRM vendor team handle them directly. You can focus on more important aspects of the entire project," Anubhav added.

"But I have a question, Bhamini, if we coordinate everything in a WhatsApp group. It will be a big chaos. How will we figure out the status of the project?" Anubhav asked.

"Every week, we send you one report called the 4P report," Bhamini said. "4P stands for Progress, Pending, Problem, and Planning," Bhamini said. "First, we send this report, and then we will have one online meeting with your Senior team to discuss all the four aspects."

"Bhamini, can you explain these 4Ps in detail, please," Anubhav asked.

"Sure, sir. The 'Progress' section will have all things completed as of yet. 'Pending' will have everything that is pending. 'Problem' is the section where we will mention problems or challenges that we are facing either on our side or from your side," Bhamini said.

"In the Planning section, we mention what we have planned for another week's time," Bhamini said. "This way, the entire process is tightly managed."

"I must say that your process is very perfectly designed. Who designed it?" Anubhav asked.

"I am not aware, Sir. But our CEO had told me that one of our earlier clients had helped design this process a few years ago," Bhamini replied.

"I think we are done with the planning for the implementation process. Let us start doing it," Liladhar said.

"I want to tell you one thing, Liladhar," Anubhav said. "You completely changed our perspective regarding the CRM implementation process. We searched for everything in the software, whereas you have shown us that we have to play an active role in the implementation. I am sure this time we will succeed."

"My mother used to say, "The relationship is like a nurse and a pregnant lady. The nurse can't deliver the baby. The baby has to be delivered by the pregnant lady. The nurse can only help to smoothen the process," Liladhar explained. "The CRM Vendor is playing the role of a nurse. They can only support you. They cannot deliver the baby. You have to deliver the baby."

Jaspreet was pleasantly surprised with the very apt example that Liladhar had given. "Awesome example, Liladhar," she said.

"Thanks," Liladhar said.

"Ah, Let me remind you of one of my favorite dialog from Deewar, an Amitabh Bachchan Movie. तुम लोग मुझे वहाँ ढूँढ रहे थे और में तुम्हारा यहाँ इंतज़ारकर रहा हूँ - You were searching for me there, while I was waiting for you here," Liladhar added.

It was already late evening, and Liladhar had to go to his hotel room and get some good rest, as he had his Yog and Ayurved session early the next morning. They all departed after promising to meet soon.

 CRM Implementation Process Secret.

The CRM vendor team is playing the role of a Nurse. They can just help you to deliver the baby. They cannot deliver the baby. It's you who is implementing the CRM. They are only helping you.

Chapter 4

· · · · · · · · · · · · · ·

Making Your Users Use CRM

सच कल्पना से भी ज़्यादा विचित्र होता है

— Vijay Singh Rajput (Amitabh Bachchan)
in the Ankhen Movie.

It's been two months since they all had last met. Today, once again, the meeting was planned by Irshad, Jagdeep, and Anubhav to discuss the issues they were facing regarding the CRM.

Liladhar was curious. The buying of CRM had gone smooth. Even the implementation was done according to the plan. What could possibly go wrong now?

With these thoughts in mind, he reached Anubhav's office. He went straight to the conference room, where the meeting was scheduled.

When he entered the conference room, Irshad and Jagdeep were already waiting there and sipping their Masala Tea. "Good Morning," Liladhar greeted them.

"Welcome, buddy, after a long time," Liladhar shook hands with both of them. While he seated and made himself comfortable, Shankar joined them. Along with him arrived the Masala tea for Liladhar also.

As usual, Anubhav was the last of the four to arrive in the office. "Old habits die hard." Jagdeep teased him when he came.

"So how is all going now? Did you want to discuss the CRM tool or something else? " Liladhar asked.

"Of course, the CRM tool," Jagdeep said.

1. What is the actual reason why your team is not using CRM?

"What now? I thought all of you were on the right track. Buying and implementing CRM both went very smoothly. What is wrong now? Is it with the software?" Liladhar asked.

Ramesh looked at Anubhav, his boss, and then he said, "I think we need some customization in the CRM, a few more reports. Also, we need to make the data entry still more user friendly."

"But why now? You had already done all the changes while in the implementation phase. You even gave a certificate of project completion to your CRM vendor. Why do you need more changes now?" Liladhar was curious.

"I think the software is not very user friendly. Our users are not able to use it properly," Anubhav said.

"What about you, guys?" Liladhar turned to Irshad and Jagdeep.

"We are not sure what the problem is, but our team is not using the CRM properly. They are not making entries," Irshad said while Jagdeep nodded in agreement.

"So, Ramesh, how do you conclude that your users are facing problems?" Liladhar asked.

"I had received various complaints from my managers and team leaders that their team members are not able to use the CRM smoothly," Ramesh said.

"Tell me one thing, how many tickets *(complaints)* have you and your team raised to the CRM vendor for those problems?" Liladhar asked.

"I don't think we have raised any tickets. Not that I can remember," Ramesh confessed.

"But, it's so easy. Your CRM app has a built-in chat system, from where you can raise the tickets and queries," Liladhar said.

"No. I don't think we have even raised the queries there," Ramesh replied.

"Ok, You had a WhatsApp group for CRM implementation. Bhamini Trivedi, the person from your CRM vendor, told you to add your entire team there. The purpose of the group was to help your users get their queries resolved. Do you see those queries in that group?" Liladhar asked once again.

"Yes, I put all the users in that group. As of now, there are 190 people in that group. Ten from Bhamini's team and 180 from our team. However, we have not received any queries from our users in that group," Ramesh said.

"In that case, how can you conclude that the problem is with CRM?" Anubhav asked Ramesh.

"I don't know exactly, but that is the only thing that I could think of," Ramesh replied.

"I would not agree with that, Ramesh," Liladhar said. "Tell me one more thing, how are your seniors using the system? Are they also facing the same issues?" he asked.

"When juniors are not using, how can seniors use the system? I mean no, they are also not using the system," Ramesh replied.

"With whatever we discussed just now, Where else do you think that the problem can be?" Liladhar said.

"But we are not sure what is the problem," Ramesh said. "We had already given them the training, given them the instructions that they need to input records properly in CRM. But still, things are not moving in the right direction."

"Let me tell you a story," Liladhar got up from his seat.

Story of a Lady searching for earrings

Once, an old lady was searching for something under the street light. Few passers saw that, and they asked her, "Mausi, what are you searching for?"

"My ear-rings," the old lady said.

Everybody who passed through that area started to help her search for the ear-ring. But even after a half-an-hour of desperately searching, they found nothing.

Then someone asked the old lady, "Where did you lose it?"

"At my home, in my hut." the old lady said. Everybody was surprised. "Then, why are you searching it here?" they asked her.

"Because there is no light at my home."

Liladhar completed his story and sat on the chair. He then asked a question to all of them "are we also searching for the ear-ring in some other place?"

Nobody replied. They were just listening and thinking. Either they had realized the problem or not yet convinced with the argument of Liladhar.

"I have seen many companies make this mistake. Even when they know that the real problem is with the users, they try to find the solution in technology," Liladhar added.

"I have a suggestion here," Jagdeep said, raising his hand. "What if we send an email and SMS to the person that their entries are pending?"

Why do Automatic escalation and gamification fail?

"How will that help?" Irshad asked.

"See, if some user does not make entries in CRM, the system will send them an email message that their entries are pending and they need to do it immediately."

"What if they don't do it even after that?" Liladhar asked.

"Then we send them another final reminder, with bold red letters, giving them the warning," Jagdeep said.

"Also, at the same time, if the entry is not done within 24 hours, we send an email to their seniors. This will create pressure on them," Shankar chimed in.

"What if they did not do anything even after the second email?" Liladhar asked.

"No, I think they will do it." Jagdeep insisted.

"Let me walk you through what will happen in this scenario," Liladhar said. "If a salesperson has 20 inquiries outstanding, he will receive 20 emails in his inbox. This number will keep increasing day by day. Twenty notifications per day will become 400 in 20 days and clutter their inbox."

"Now, since they are smart people, will they not create a rule and a folder in the email client? So, all the email notifications from the CRM will go directly to that folder and don't clutter the inbox," Liladhar said.

"Hmm, that is possible," Irshad said.

"Also, just think of what will happen with the seniors," Liladhar continued. "Say a sales manager has ten people on the team reporting to them. How many email notifications will they receive? More importantly, will they also not create the rule and a folder to declutter their inbox?"

"Yes, agreed. This system won't work." Anubhav said.

"Also, Jagdeep, as a boss, just think what will happen to your inbox. How many notifications will you receive when your team does not perform the task of using CRM?" Liladhar asked.

"Ok. Ok. I got it." Jagdeep said in a confession tone.

"Here's a thumb rule to remember before you implement any feature or change any feature in CRM: Play chess and not ludo. Always think of the next few steps," Liladhar said.

"Hmm. I liked that idea. Playing chess and thinking about what will happen next. In fact, this discussion saved us from falling into the 'notification' trap," Anubhav added.

But we are not able to find the solution to this problem. How do we get our users to use the CRM properly? Why are they not using the CRM tool?" Jagdeep surrendered but under a protest.

"Yes, why are they not using the CRM?" Irshad asked. "Is it because they think that this is extra work?"

When your team knows you are not serious about the CRM tool

"The main reason why your team members are not using the CRM tool is that they know that you are not serious about it," Liladhar said. "They think that CRM is one of those Saturday-evening-party-bubbles. You might have met someone, so you are doing all this. But it will fade away in a few days."

Irshad seemed to be very upset at all this. "I don't understand all this. You are telling that our team thinks that we are not serious about them using the CRM? How do we let them know that we are serious about CRM?"

"If we would not have been serious, why would we spend so much time and money on the CRM! Of course, we are serious," Jagdeep protested.

"How many of you sitting in this room have installed the CRM app on your mobiles?" Liladhar asked.

"I was the first person in our company to install it," Ramesh said. "Since I had to do the testing part."

"I have installed the app but not logged into it yet," Irshad gave a sheepish smile.

Jagdeep had not even installed the App. Anubhav had installed the app and was very happy that he was not amongst the ones who did pass the test.

"Does this give you a hint as to what is wrong with the CRM?" Liladhar asked.

"Let us discover more points. How have you been doing your sales reviews with your teams since the CRM got implemented? Especially how do you get the data for the review meetings? What do you use for reporting." Liladhar asked.

 The actual reason why your team is not using CRM.

Your team knows that you are not serious about them using CRM. Do not allow other channels of reporting, like WhatsApp, email, or Spreadsheet. Always conduct review meetings with CRM only. Have discussions with your team to discuss what problems they are facing with CRM.

Why parallel reporting kills the CRM

"Review meetings are regular. But we are still using our old Excel files and reports submitted by salespersons on the email," Ramesh said. Anubhav nodded in agreement.

"Same with us, we are still using our old reporting structure only," Jagdeep said. Irshad also shared the same status.

"There is a famous quote by Eliyahu Goldratt, who wrote the book "The Goal." *Tell me how you measure me, and I will tell you how I will behave. If you measure me in an illogical way... do not complain about illogical behavior...*" Liladhar said. "If you still keep accepting WhatsApp and Excel reports, your people will keep on giving you the same. No wonder," Liladhar continued.

"I told you, your team knows that you are not serious about the CRM. You are showing that with all the actions that you are doing," Liladhar added.

"In that case, what do you suggest we should do?" Jagdeep asked.

"First of all, do not respond or give instructions on WhatsApp. You have the CRM for that. If some salesperson is updating something on WhatsApp, ask them whether they have updated the CRM or not," Liladhar replied.

"Let us discuss one more thing. Tell me how many times you called your team in person or call and told them that you want everything to be done in CRM?" Liladhar asked.

"We had sent them an email, a broadcast from the CEO's desk," Ramesh replied. "Apart from that, we had also informed them while CRM training was happening."

2. How to let your team know that you are serious about CRM

"Let me share how I conveyed to my team that I am serious about our CRM," Liladhar said. "It looks a little complicated, but it works for sure."

He continued, "This was a few years ago when we had just started to use the CRM. Back then, we used to have nine people in our Sales team. We did not have any sales manager. I was handling that responsibility."

"We had decided that we wanted to capture a deal-wise gross profit (GP). So, we added one more field in our opportunities module to capture that information for every deal, to prioritize our sales efforts easily." Liladhar said. "This was on a Monday morning; we all sat in our conference room. We explained why we need that information, how to make entries, and so on."

"After detailed training, I asked everybody if anyone had any doubts. I also got a positive nod from everyone that they had understood everything and will make those changes without fail. Anyways, it was a tiny task, as they all already knew how to calculate GP." Liladhar continued.

"Did that work?" Jagdeep was getting impatient.

"I bet you will be surprised. This meeting happened on Monday morning. On Monday afternoon, I had to go to Malaysia for a business trip. So on Tuesday morning, when I checked our CRM app on my mobile, no one had done any entry. All the deals records had an empty GP field," Liladhar said.

"See, I told you. This problem is everywhere." Ramesh said. "But what did you do then?" He was curious to know.

"From my hotel room in Malaysia, I called each of our salespersons and asked them what the challenge was and why they could not do it. I got a variety of different reasons and excuses from them. All of them promised that they will do it from now onwards," Liladhar said.

"But, I did not take their promise. I told them to do those changes while I hold the call." Liladhar continued. "That day, I spent around 1 hour in calling all these people and getting those changes done."

"Ok, I see. Maybe we can try this idea. Ask them to do it, then and there, while we wait," Jagdeep said.

"Imagine what happened on Wednesday morning?" Liladhar asked. "Out of nine, only four people had done the proper entries for Tuesday. So, once again, I called those five people and went through my previous day's routine."

"On Thursday morning, out of nine, three people had not yet done those entries. So I had to call these three people again on Thursday," Liladhar said.

"They might have felt pretty embarrassed because of this," Anubhav said. He was starting to get the secret sauce, but not yet fully.

"On Friday, however, only one person had not done things properly. So I had to make just one call. I asked him whether he wanted to continue the job or not, since everyone was doing things properly, and he was the only person left," Liladhar continued.

"Do you mean we should call daily to all our team members and beg to make these entries?" Irshad was furious.

"No. Not at all. Till today, after that Friday, I have never had to request to make use of CRM properly," Liladhar said. "It's about letting your team know that you are serious about something."

"Hmm, I think I get it now. It's about converting it into a habit." Anubhav said thoughtfully.

"More importantly, it's about letting them know that you are serious about CRM. You are committed, and you can go to any extent for this." Liladhar concluded. "That is what I conveyed to them when I called each of them daily."

"I like this idea. I think this is one of the best culture-building tips that I have learned till today. This way, you never have to get upset. But you get your work done," Irshad said. He seemed to have found the Aladdin's lamp now.

 Let your team know that you are serious about CRM.

Most sales managers and bosses think that if they send one email or give instructions once, their team will do exactly as you had instructed them. But that does not work. Do a proper follow up a few times. If they are facing problems, get them solved. They will not be able to give excuses for a long time.

Our people are like our kids

"Let me share one more secret. Our people are like our kids. No, I am not making an emotional statement. It's a pure psychological fact. Our kids don't do what we tell them to do; they do what we do. The same is true with our people also," Liladhar said.

"Yes, as it is said - practice, don't preach," Shankar added.

"But, it is easier said than done," Liladhar added.

"If you don't use CRM, you cannot expect your team to use CRM. It's ok if you are too busy, you don't make all the entries. But at least you can see the reports and dashboards regularly," Liladhar said.

"Will that bring a change in the team member's mentality?" Irshad asked.

"Yes, definitely," Liladhar said. "If the boss is looking at their work, it's a great motivation for people."

"I have seen people complain as to; What is the use of making entries? Anyway, no one is checking it," Liladhar said.

"Yes, I agree. This sounds logical to me," Jagdeep said.

"How many times did you talk to the person who is not using the system? What problem were they facing while using the CRM?" Liladhar asked. "I suggest that if they are not using the system, talk to them, and don't get upset. Just ask them what the problem is."

"I think there can be one more problem," Shankar said. "Maybe they are not comfortable with transparency. They feel their privacy is in danger."

"This is a very normal feeling any person can have. This is the reason I have been telling you all not to see the CRM as a reporting tool," Liladhar said. "Perception management is critical," Liladhar added.

"Aha, I like that word - perception management. I thought it was useful only in politics. But you are right. If we don't create the perception properly, people will build their own perception. Which can be dangerous." Jagdeep said.

"A CRM is not going to attack the privacy of the users. But you will have to discuss that problem in detail with your team members." Liladhar added.

"Yes, I think we have got the root cause of the problem. We will work towards that. Like charity, change also begins from home," Anubhav said.

"There is also a nice little trick you can use to save your time and, at the same time, convey your team about your CRM intentions," Liladhar said. "But this simple trick will change the way your entire team is looking towards the CRM."

"What is that?" Jagdeep asked.

How to use 'CRM-Notifications' effectively?

"You all know that CRM has the capability of sending notifications to the users on mobile, web, email, or even SMS." Liladhar started to explain.

"Now, there is a concept of Owner-Notification. In which the user, who is the owner of a particular record, gets a notification when someone else comments on that record." Liladhar continued. "So If I, as your manager, comment on an opportunity assigned to you, you will get a notification."

"But, how can that be useful in user adoption?" Anubhav asked.

"In fact, It is one of the most powerful ways of getting user-adoption," Liladhar added. "Suppose team leaders or bosses spend 20 minutes daily on their mobile, analyzing the Leads and opportunities which their team members are working on, and they comment on those records and give their feedback, suggestions, and remarks. It will send an email notification to the user that their boss has recently added the comment to their Opportunity." Liladhar continued. "What effect, do you think, that email will create?"

"Hmm, it sounds like a good idea. Now the users will know that their boss is checking their work." Ramesh added.

"Yes, Ramesh. But that is not the main benefit," Liladhar said. "The main benefit is Information-Experience exchange, that happens this way."

Jagdeep said, "Explain, please."

"See, your salespeople have lots of information about the customer and also about the deal. This is natural as they are the people who are in touch with the customer. At the same time, Sales managers, team leaders, and bosses have lots of experience, as they have invested lots of years in the sales field." Liladhar said.

"Just imagine, what would happen if all the information that is available with the salesperson is available to the Sales Managers and at the same time, the Sales Managers can share their experience with the salesperson," Liladhar continued.

"Wow, I never imagined that we could use this feature this way," Jagdeep said with excitement.

"Shankar, now tell me. Will your salespeople still have a problem with transparency?" Liladhar asked. To which Shankar replied, "I am sure this will change their outlook."

"Actually, there is another benefit of using the owner-notification function. It's a much bigger and long-term benefit," Liladhar said.

 Exchange of Information and Experience.

Sales executives have a lot of information about the deals they are working on, whereas Sales managers have a lot of experience. To achieve maximum efficiency in the sales process, Salesteam should exchange this information and experience regularly. The Owner-Notification feature of CRM is precisely meant for this.

Jagdeep asked, "What is that function?"

"Now that you have understood how it works, give me some examples of comments that you would put on opportunities records in the CRM. What comments, suggestions, or instructions would you pass to your team?" Liladhar asked.

"Sometimes, we know the particular customer is a hard negotiator, so we can comment on the salesperson to take care in pricing, as the customer will do a hard negotiation," Irshad said.

"Also, if the customer has a bad credit reputation, we can inform the sales team," Jagdeep added.

"It may also happen that I have some high-level connections with the top management, where my sales team is following a deal. I can offer them help if they need it. That will help them close the deal faster," Anubhav added, as he was proud of his influential background.

"Sometimes, if some deal is stuck at some point due to negotiation dead-lock, we can ask the salesperson to give a discount and close the deal. This happens when the customer is prestigious, and we need them anyhow," Irshad said.

"In fact, there will be a lot of other things that you can do. But tell me one thing what message it gives to the salespersons. Does it sound like monitoring or helping hand?" Liladhar asked.

"Sure, it is a great help to the salesperson," Irshad replied.

"Also, it's a great learning experience for the entire sales team. I think, even if we use this one feature, we get paisa-vasool *(full value for our money)*." Jagdeep said.

"Do you think this is a good reason for your team to start using the CRM?" Liladhar asked.

"Yes, of course," Anubhav said. "We will have to do a detailed session regarding this with our sales team. We have to convince them regarding this. Ramesh, make sure that we arrange a meeting. I will personally attend that meeting and convince all the sales leaders."

"Hmm, Liladhar, Now I got your secret. Now I know what you do in those 20 minutes daily morning," Jagdeep smiled.

"Liladhar, how can we give them a few more reasons to start using CRM?" Shankar asked.

"There is a straightforward way to do it," Liladhar replied. "Just create templates for them. They would start loving the CRM."

Email, SMS & WhatsApp templates increase CRM usage

"What templates?" Irshad asked.

"All your salespersons communicate with your clients and prospects by email, SMS, and WhatsApp. But currently, they are doing it in their own way. What if you provide a template for each and everything that they are sending?" Liladhar explained.

"Hmm, that sounds interesting," Irshad said. "But what templates should we make?"

Irshad continued with more questions "Who will make these templates? Can't we get sample templates from the CRM Vendor and use them?"

"Go slow, go slow.One question at a time," Liladhar smiled.

"There are lots of things that can be templatized. Your corporate introduction, product information, service related information. In fact, you can think of many more things," Liladhar continued.

"Which means we can have templates for Bank account, address and company taxation details also," Jagdeep said.

"Yes, why not. In fact, everything that needs to be sent more than once can be and should be templatized," Liladhar added.

"Should we have templates for Email only or SMS and WhatsApp also?" Irshad asked.

"Why not, you can surely have all. Templatization has lots of advantages," Liladhar continued. "Communication is standardized; the quality of communication is maintained, and people spend less time thinking and more time doing. CRM can templatize 65% of communication done by the sales team. It will save more than 25% of their time spent on writing messages." Liladhar said.

"Our CRM tool also has a report which shows an analysis of how many times the templates have been used," Shankar added.

"Wow, that's a great feature," Jagdeep said. "But the question remains, who will create the templates?"

"Jagdeep, since you have a small team, just call a team meeting for 30 minutes and you can create templates during the session. The presence of all your team members will also increase the sense of participation," Liladhar said.

"Shankar, you, please get all the team leaders for a small meeting and get this template thing rolled out, ASAP!" Anubhav instructed Ramesh.

"Sure, Sir, consider it done," Ramesh replied.

 Messages Templates improve user adoption.

You can templatize 65% of the communication that your salespeople make. If templates are appropriately used, they can save up to 25% of the time spent on creating and sending messages over SMS, WhatsApp, and Email.

"Liladhar, last month, one of our salespeople left the organization. The new person has not yet joined. So all the records are still assigned to the outgoing person only. I had a question. Is there a specific policy which we should use when anyone leaves or joins the team?" Ramesh asked.

"Yes, there is. But before we discuss that, we have to keep in mind two things. Firstly, we need to understand the type of records in the CRM because the assignment will happen based on the type of records," Liladhar replied and then paused.

"What is the other thing?" Jagdeep asked.

"The second thing is that now I need some more tea," Liladhar said.

"Of course," Ramesh said as he picked up the intercom to order the special masala tea for all of them.

3. What you should do when people change (leave or join)

"the biggest mistake that people make is that they don't reassign the records when a person leaves the organization. This creates ghost entries. There will be lots of opportunities and tickets, to which no one is attending." Liladhar said.

"Some of the records assigned to the outgoing person leaving the organization have to be assigned to the new incoming person taking charge. But let us first understand that there are three types of records in a CRM," Liladhar started his explanation.

"There are Master Records, like companies, persons, products. These records are long-term information about your clients. You should assign all the records assigned to the outgoing person to the new person joining in, or to the person taking charge of those clients," Liladhar said.

"Then there are transaction records like Leads, opportunities, Tickets, Quotations, Contracts. Here is a little trick. Don't change any old records, which are already closed. But all the pending, open, ongoing records should be assigned to the new person, who is taking charge."

"Why is there a different treatment for these records?" Jagdeep asked.

"Because you need to know who has closed those leads or tickets. Also, the pending work to be assigned to the new person. Actually, this is what you exactly do physically also. When a person leaves, generally, there is a hand-over process. Where all the pending work is assigned to the new person," Liladhar explained.

"But in our case, the new person has not yet joined. What should we do then in the CRM?" Ramesh asked.

"What will you do outside the CRM? Will some other people handle the opportunities that this person has been handling?" Liladhar asked. "Or will you wait till someone joins the company?"

"Of course, his senior colleague will handle it. Our customer cannot wait till we hire a new person," Anubhav added, interrupting Ramesh before he could try to answer.

"Then you have to do the same thing in the CRM also. Assign those open opportunities to his Senior colleague," Liladhar replied.

"But then all the records will get mixed. When a new person joins, how do we know which records we have to assign to him?" Ramesh asked.

First, Liladhar stared at Ramesh with the question mark, then he replied, "Simple, just ask this question to Bhamini, your CRM success officer. She will tell you. But let me give you a hint."

"In every CRM, there is a concept of TAGs. You can tag the records which you need to identify," Liladhar said. "Ask your CRM vendor team to help you with it."

"Oh, I am sorry for asking such a simple question. I could have thought of this," Ramesh said.

"No problem, Ramesh. More importantly, I want to point out that to all of you. Just take your problems to your CRM vendors. They will definitely have a way out," Liladhar said.

"What are the third type of records?" Irshad brought the discussion back on track.

"The third type of records are activities, Calls, SMS, Emails, Meetings, visits, etc. You don't have to do anything for these records," Liladhar added.

"I am more worried about what we do when a new person joins the organization since we plan to hire a couple of new people next month. What do we do then?" Irshad asked.

"Of course, you need to arrange a CRM training from the vendor," replied Ramesh. "It is one of the primary responsibilities of the CRM Admin to get all the team members appropriately trained."

"Yes, but before that, you need to train the person in the process first. Remember, CRM is a part of your entire sales process, not the entire process. This is one of the most common misunderstandings that people have," Liladhar said.

"You had asked about how we are doing sales review meetings. Can you explain to us what should be the best way to do Sales review meetings?" Anubhav asked.

4. Always do Sales Review and CRM review simultaneously

"There are many books and theories on how Sales review meetings should be held. So, it would be better if we get some sales consultants to speak on the same," Liladhar said.

"Yes, bhai, I understand that. But I mean, we all want to understand how you use CRM to conduct your sales review meetings,' Anubhav said.

"Before we discuss that, let me tell you one thumb-rule here. We should always do sales reviews based on real data from CRM. I have seen many companies who use CRM, but they create spreadsheets and then discuss that for reviews. This is a wrong method and prone to many errors of omission," Liladhar said.

"But what is the problem with spreadsheets?" Ramesh said. "As we already have our reports formats ready there. Also, our teams know how to make those reports."

"Ramesh, we already discussed that we have to abandon other reporting structures if we want to implement CRM. Why are you again going back on the old track," Anubhav told Ramesh and signaled Liladhar to continue.

"Reason is straightforward. If we allow people to create figures for the reports, there are also chances of errors and sometimes manipulation. Further, you cannot drill-down in the reports created in spreadsheets." Liladhar said.

"Agreed," Jagdeep said.

"Ok, First of all, let us understand why we have sales review meetings," Liladhar posed the question.

"To make sure whether the sales team is on the right track or not. Whether they are reaching their targets or not," Irshad said.

"To review how they are working, if there are any issues, then help them correct it," Jagdeep added.

"To update Sales team leaders with the numbers," Ramesh said. Anubhav thought that almost everything was covered, so he just passed the question.

"Ok, so here are some ideas from what we have been doing, " Liladhar said. "In the initial days of CRM adoption, not just sales numbers, but even the CRM data needs analysis."

"What does that mean?" Jagdeep asked.

"When you move to the CRM, in the initial days, there will be plenty of mistakes in using it. Such as selecting the wrong sales-stage, missing amount, or missing update about a particular deal's progress. *Sales review meetings should also be a CRM usage review*," Liladhar explained.

"But, will that not deviate the sales review meeting into all kinds of CRM support related questions?" Ramesh asked his doubt.

"No. Absolutely not. I mean, if the CRM Admin has done a proper job, then this will not happen," Liladhar replied.

"Also, if the issues are found, then the team member should be asked to correct it immediately in the meeting. This will give one more signal to the team members that the management is serious about the CRM," Liladhar.

"Yes, this seems to be a good idea, as lots of issues and problems will get resolved then and there," Anubhav said.

"Further, if we use the Owner-notification feature and if all the sales team leaders keep a check on the records and data in the CRM, then there is no need for a review meeting to update the leadership about the numbers. Everybody is aware of the numbers," Liladhar said.

"Also, since the sales managers are getting updated about the deals on a daily basis, they need not wait for the weekly or fortnightly sales review meeting. So these meetings can be utilized for some higher purposes," Liladhar continued.

"What higher purposes?" Jagdeep asked.

"Before the CRM, you were using the meeting to discuss what happened. Now with the CRM, you already know what happened, So you can use the meeting to discuss why it happened,," Liladhar said.

 Always do Sales Review meetings with real CRM Data.

Using CRM dashboards and reports for sales review meetings will ensure three things. First, the users will have to put their data in the CRM compulsorily. Second, you get accurate data live from the CRM. Finally, as you do a sales review, you can drill-down the reports for more details.

"I think there is one more benefit of Sales review meetings with a CRM. We get a chance to go deeper into any deal instantly. We get to know more details about the deals immediately. It will make meetings more transparent," Irshad said.

"There can be lots of things that you can do with that extra time that gets saved. But there is no point in discussing those here. You will have to do this practice with your sales team," Liladhar said.

"In my company, our sales review meetings start and end with the CRM on the screen only. Believe me; we have some of the shortest and more effective sales review meetings. We are able to easily find what is wrong rather than discussing who is wrong,," Liladhar added.

"This is a useful idea. I am sure it will benefit us," Irshad said.

Jagdeep had something in mind which was troubling him. "As you helped us uncover the hidden secrets about the reporting and Sales review meeting. We would like to know your opinion and understanding of CRM reporting."

"Yes, what would you like to know?" Liladhar asked.

"How, according to you, should we use the CRM reporting structure to manage our teams in the best possible way?" Jagdeep asked.

5. Philosophy of reporting and analysis from CRM

"Before we discuss reporting, let us understand that reporting in any system is done for proper diagnosis. Perhaps the best diagnosis system is found in Ayurved," Liladhar started to explain.

"But have you ever seen a vaid *(An Ayurvedic Doctor)* who just holds your hand for around 60 seconds?" Liladhar asked them

"Yes, I have seen. Actually, my dad never went to an allopathic doctor; he had always gone to an Ayurvedic doctor only," Jagdeep remembered his dad fondly. "It looks like they measure the pulse."

"Actually, it is much deeper. It is called Nadi-Parikshan or Pulse diagnosis. Although we translate Nadi to pulse, the actual meaning is different. Pulse is just the palpation in any place of the body. Whereas Nadi is a term used for all the channels through which the energy flows," Liladhar explained.

"Looks like a class in Ayurved, but it is Interesting. I am always interested in Indian Tradition," Irshad said.

"Did you know that a vaid, after holding your hand for 60 seconds, can tell you a lot of things about what you ate, how you slept yesterday, or even ailments which have been around for years?" Liladhar asked.

"If we go a little deeper, what they are measuring is not a pulse, but they measure seven different parameters with three fingers. A combination of different parameters helps them to diagnose so effectively," Liladhar said.

Ayurvedic principle of See, touch, and ask

"Don't worry, and we don't need to understand the details. What I want to say here is the philosophy behind this diagnosis. It's called DSP which means, Darshanam *(see)*, sparsham *(touch)*, prashnam *(ask)*." Liladhar continued.

"Wow, that is interesting," Irshad said.

"First, the *Vaid* sees the patient, observes them. Second, they touch them, which is they do the Nadi-parikshan, and third, they ask questions if required," Liladhar said. "If we follow the same policy for reporting, we will be able to get much more information in a very minimum effort."

"But, there is a catch here. Sales managers and bosses need to learn how to read numbers. They should know the deep connections between numbers, and should be able to draw conclusions and relationships between different numbers," Liladhar added.

"Yes, you are right, then only we will be able to diagnose the problems properly," Irshad said.

"Hmm. Liladhar Shastri, I must say that your fees for the Ayurved class have been a full paisa-vasool. I am impressed with this fresh perspective on reporting, using Ancient Indian concepts." Anubhav said, with full excitement in his eyes.

"I call it AI-based reporting. AI, as in, Ancient Indian wisdom," Liladhar concluded. "Now, let us come back to CRM reporting."

"So, even for the CRM reporting to be effective, we can follow these three DSP principles. First, we see the report, then drill down more if required, and then we ask relevant questions to relevant people to get to the root of the issue," Liladhar continued.

"Basically, Whatever we want to learn from a CRM can be divided into two things. First, status updates, where we want to be updated about the latest status. Second, a detailed analysis of things that have happened or are happening," Liladhar started to explain again.

Dashboards and reports

"So, on a day-to-day basis or in real-time, we use the dashboard to get status updates. However, we use analytical reports for forensic analysis of what happened. We might need these reports a few times in a week or a month," Liladhar added.

"That's fine, but what is the difference between a dashboard and an analytical report?" Irshad asked. "Do you mean that anything graphical is a dashboard and anything detailed is a report?"

"No. It has got nothing to do with how it is represented," Liladhar said. "A dashboard generally gives you an at-a-glance view of key performance indicators. It may be graphical or just a bunch of numbers."

"Can you give us some examples? We get what you are saying, but I think a few examples will help us digest it properly," Jagdeep said.

"Ok, you use the dashboard to know things like leads generated, leads status, and open opportunities. Generally, dashboards will answer your questions regarding how, what, who, where, when," Liladhar said.

"Whereas when you want to understand questions relating to 'why,' you will get to detailed reporting. Analytical reports are something which you will use to go deeper." Liladhar added.

"What can be an example of an analytical report?" Jagdeep asked.

"For example, comparative analysis of two years sales winning ratio, a periodic report regarding how much time was spent on each stage in the opportunity," Liladhar explained.

"There is one more way to differentiate between the dashboard and detailed reports. Dashboards are useful for monitoring, tracking, or supervision the processes or teams. Whereas detailed reports are useful for detailed forensic analysis." Liladhar said.

"That means we will need a dashboard for daily reporting and monitoring. Also, maybe in initial periods, we will need dashboards for increasing the user-adoption. Once our users start using the CRM properly, then maybe our detailed reports will help us." Jagdeep added.

"Exactly, you are correct. We should never look at analytical reports at very short intervals. Otherwise, the whole purpose gets defeated." Liladhar added. "Take an example of your pulse as a dashboard and your blood report as an analytical report. You may monitor pulse a few times a day, but you do blood reports only a few times a year."

 Dashboards and analytical reports.

Dashboards are meant for daily and regular monitoring purposes, whereas analytical reports are used periodically, often weekly or monthly, to do a much more in-depth analysis. There is no point in wasting energy on analytical reports daily.

"Liladhar, I feel that you should write a book on how principles of Ancient Yog and Ayurved can be used in modern business management," Anubhav said.

"You know what? I am also thinking about the same. In fact, Yog and Ayurved will always remain modern and evergreen. The principles in them and knowledge are timeless." Liladhar said.

"Great. I wish you all the luck with your book." Anubhav said. "I want to ask one more question: is there a report which tells us that our users are using the CRM properly or not," Anubhav asked? "So that we can be sure that we are on the right track."

"Rather than getting one report to check on your own, it's always a better idea to get your CRM Audit done every 60 days, by an expert from your CRM Vendor," Liladhar said.

"CRM Audit, But how will it help? What do they know about your business? Are they spying on our data? Do they charge us separately?" Irshad had too many questions.

6. Why a CRM Audit every 60 days is a must

"Hold on, dear, one question at a time," Liladhar said. "Firstly, CRM Audit is not a one-time event; it's a process that needs to be done regularly, generally every 60 days."

"Will they send us an Audit Report?" Irshad asked.

"No. It's not a report. Basically, it's a process. All your senior team members should be present in the Audit session. So they get first-hand information as to what needs improvement." Liladhar said. "If you just get a report, then it is going to be of no use."

"The entire Audit process is done based on dashboards and reports in your CRM. Actually, you can also do the Audit on your own. But having a CRM vendor doing it has more effect on our team members," Liladhar continued.

"I agree. When an outsider shows us something, it has more effect on our team members," Ramesh said. "BTW, what does it cover?"

Usage Analysis, Data Quality Analysis, and Process Quality Analysis

"A CRM audit helps you in more than one way. It helps you to know whether (a) Usage Analysis. (b) DQA - Data Quality Analysis. (c) PQA - Process Quality Analysis," Liladhar added.

"It looks like a complete audit, rather than just a CRM software Audit," Jagdeep said.

"Yes, definitely. Usage analysis will tell you about your team's usage of the CRM system, whether they are using it properly or not. It will also inform you if there are some CRM features that you are not using," Liladhar added.

"I see that there is a hidden benefit of Usage Analysis. We will discover lots of useful features, which have been unused. We can start using them," Ramesh said.

"You are right," Liladhar added. "Any CRM is as good as the quality of data in it. CRM data needs to be correct, complete, and consistent. Data Quality Analysis will help you understand gaps in data that your team has been adding to the system while using it."

"There are various DQA reports in CRM, which come by default, which you will understand in this section of the CRM audit," Liladhar added. "Lot of data, when seen in relation to each other, starts making more sense. You will learn these techniques in the DQA section."

"That's good. So, once we understand those reports, maybe we can do those checks more frequently. We can do it ourselves to improve the data quality," Ramesh added.

"The ultimate goal of deploying a CRM system is to have proper processes. PQA or process Quality Analysis will help you take a deep dive into this. For example: are your team members converting leads properly or not? Are they following the qualification process?," Liladhar said.

"I think the PQA will be most useful of all," Anubhav said.

"Yes, definitely. But PQA will come only after DQA and usage analysis. There is no point indulging in PQA unless your CRM usage and data quality are proper," Liladhar said.

"One more thing. There is one more secret benefit of getting a CRM audit done," Liladhar said.

Jagdeep started to grow impatient now, "What is that?"

"A CRM audit is the best way to clear CRM-related doubts of your team members. Because everyone will be in that meeting, we also have a senior representative from the CRM vendor," Liladhar explained.

"Wow, that looks like a real secret gem," Jagdeep smiled.

"BTW, you don't need to worry about the privacy matter during the CRM Audit. Everything is covered under NDA that you have signed with the CRM Vendor," Liladhar said.

"Almost everything is now clear, except for one thing," Anubhav asked. "We are not yet clear as to how we can manage the Sales Targets in the CRM."

"Sure, but this topic requires a little elaborate discussion. Let us finish lunch first."

"But today, we are not getting lunch here. In fact, we are going to Madras Cafe, the most famous south Indian restaurant in Mumbai." Anubhav told everybody.

"Ok, Thalaiva *(the boss),*" said Liladhar as everybody moved out of the conference room to head for the restaurant.

7. Sales target management in CRM

The four of them returned to the conference room after lunch.

"Let me tell you one thing that I like about meeting all of you for your CRM project," Liladhar said.

"Yes, Please," Jagdeep said.

"Every time there is awesome food. I am loving it," Liladhar replied. "When we left, we were discussing sales target management in CRM. I would like to ask you how do you define the target and how do you measure the targets."

"In our case, it is simple, we have sales targets per person in amount per month, for every salesperson," Jagdeep said.

Sales target-incentive is tricky

"We have one more parameter added to the sales target. That is a type of product. Some slow-moving items in agriculture equipment are highly profitable and some low margin high moving items. Obviously, targets and incentives depend based on that." Irshad said.

"In our case, it's a little complex. Since we are into products and projects. So we have different target mechanisms for both teams. Also, since we work with multiple vendors, we have vendor-specific targets also." Anubhav said. "Ramesh, am I missing anything."

"Yes, Sir. We also have geography-specific targets." Ramesh said.

"Oh, yes. I missed it. When we want to promote sales in specific geographies, we create targets accordingly," Anubhav added.

"Ok, so all of you have different requirements for managing targets. That's pretty complex. I have one more question for you. You might also have an incentive or penalty system when targets are achieved or not achieved," Liladhar said.

"Yes, of course, we have different percentages of incentives on different brands and different categories of products. Also, we have based the incentive system based on payment collection. If payment is in time, then they get the full incentive. The incentive reduces as payment is delayed," Anubhav added.

"That makes it even more complex," Liladhar added. "What about you, guys?" Liladhar asked Jagdeep and Irshad.

"In our case, the incentive is a standard percentage." Jagdeep clarified.

"We have a product category based incentive structure," Irshad added.

"Are there any more layers that I should know about?" Liladhar asked.

"Yes, the targets are monthly and quarterly. Then there is the average monthly target, which is based on yearly performance. Based on that yearly incentive, or bonus is calculated," Anubhav added.

"Wow, that makes it super complex," Liladhar said. "I think there might be one more layer of complication. You might also have targets for sales managers and their teams?"

"Yes, we do have Sales managers have a different target for themselves and their teams. Their incentive is based on a formula which involves the achievement of both the targets," Anubhav said.

Liladhar seemed to be expecting this kind of complication. "How do you manage targets and incentives as of now."

"Liladhar, it's a very complex mechanism," Shankar interrupted. He was involved in creating those complex Excel spreadsheets, which had so many formulae that no one understood. "We have a set of few spreadsheets, where we put the data to calculate the targets."

"You mean you don't have one spreadsheet that calculates everything," Liladhar asked.

"I hope all of you are getting the level of complication which you are expecting from the CRM system," Liladhar said.

"Spreadsheets are supposed to be a flexible piece of software as you can add any formula anywhere and change the format whenever you want. However, that is not possible in a structured software like a CRM, where the database structure is predetermined," Liladhar continued.

"Now you have a complex calculation which even the spreadsheet is not able to make. How on earth do you think that the CRM software can do it?" Liladhar added.

"Tell me one more thing. Does your target and incentive structure change?" Liladhar asked all of them.

"Yes, quite often. Sometimes it is from our vendors, sometimes because of market demands. But the target structure and rates both keep on changing," Anubhav said.

Jagdeep and Irshad did not have a complex target-incentive system, but they would still have preferred the system's flexibility.

"That makes it almost impossible to develop a software system to manage this," Liladhar said. "At least, at a reasonable cost. If you are ready to spend a bomb, you can get it developed. How much would you spend? This is the reason that no CRM in the world has a perfect sales target management system," Liladhar added.

"Do you mean there could be an extra cost for the target module?" Anubhav asked.

"I am not a CRM vendor. But from what we discussed, it seems like a huge task. Obviously, it cannot come for free or for a very low cost," Liladhar replied.

How much focus should you keep on target?

"Then what should we do? Because I think target v/s achieved is one of the most important parameters for our sales team. In fact, I think that whenever our sales team opens their mobile or web apps, they should see a chart which shows targets v/s achieved," Ramesh said.

"So that they are always motivated," Ramesh added.

"Do you think that is motivating or scary? Imagine when you were a student, what if your mother kept on reminding you every time you have to get 95% marks," Liladhar asked.

Before waiting for the answer, he continued.

"I have a question for all of you," Liladhar said. "Suppose you want to go from Mumbai to Delhi by car. You put the destination as Delhi on GPS, and then you start driving."

"Now, you have to keep an eye on GPS so that you don't miss your directions. But at the same time, you also have to keep attention to driving the car safely on the road. You have to make sure that you follow all the driving rules and regulations," Liladhar said.

"Now the question is what is more important, GPS, or driving safely as per rules. Where you should put more attention?" Liladhar asked.

"Of course, we will keep our eye on the road and make sure that we drive safely and as per rules. That is more important. But at the same time, we have to keep an eye on the GPS screen also," Ramesh replied.

"You are right. Let me extend the question. How often would you see GPS, and how often do you keep an eye on the road?" Liladhar asked again.

"We will keep a continuous eye on the road, but whenever there is a turn or diversion on the road, we will look at the GPS screen," Ramesh replied. "Wait a minute, do you mean to say that GPS is like our Sales target?"

Anubhav seemed to have got the hint where this was going, so he interrupted Ramesh and said to Liladhar, "Ok. I get it. We should not be solely focused on the sales-targets, but then what should we have an eye on? What should we monitor continuously?" he asked.

"For that, let me ask you another question. Suppose you want to reduce weight. Where do you keep your eye on? What would you measure all the time? Your weight, or what you eat, and how much do you work-out?"

"Of course, we need to focus on what we eat and how much we work-out. The change in weight is the final outcome. It is the result of the activities we do and how much and what food we eat" Jagdeep replied.

"Now, I am getting it. It sound something similar to that famous sloka (verse) from Bhagwad Geeta - कर्मण्येवाधिकारस्ते मा फलेषु कदाचन - You have the right to work only but never to its fruits. Don't focus on the results; focus on your work or duty," Irshad said with excitement.

"Yes, you are 100% right. By the way, it is *slok* and not sloka." Liladhar said. "Hope you all got an idea, as to what you need to keep an eye on?" he asked.

"No." Jagdeep said, "Explain, please."

"Yes, Liladhar, I want you to explain a little deeper about this," Anubhav said.

"I would strongly recommend one book to all of you. ***Cracking the Sales Management Code, By Jason Jordan and Michelle Vazzana***. This is one of the best books on Sales Management," Liladhar said.

"Ok, Boss. We will get the book. But now you, please explain to us in short," Anubhav teased Liladhar.

"There are three types of metrics that we find in sales management. Sales results, sales activities, and sales objectives," Liladhar explained.

"Sales results metrics are metrics like sales achieved; payment collected sales achieved v/s targets, etc.. These metrics cannot be directly managed by sales managers or sales teams. In fact, they are the end results of Sales activities," Liladhar continued.

"Sales activities are the second type of metrics. Activities consist of everything our sales team does. Calls, meetings, sending emails, creating proposals, giving demos, giving presentations, attending sales training, etc. Salespeople can manage these activities," Liladhar said.

"Hmm, that makes sense. We can increase the number of visits or number of calls done or quotations submitted, which will, in turn, change the sales results. But what are sales objectives?" Anubhav asked.

"Sales objectives come in between the Sales results and sales activities. They are not actual end-results but the objectives or goals that you set to achieve the result." Liladhar replied.

Jagdeep said, "Could you give us some examples?"

"Examples of sales objectives are the percentage of customer retention, Number of customers acquired. Percentage of wallet of the customer, Customer satisfaction index, etc. Does this make sense?" Liladhar asked Jagdeep.

"Yes, somewhat. now, it is exciting." Jagdeep replied.

Targets should be on sales results, sales activities, and sales objectives

"So now, if we come back to the target management topic. Don't you think that we should have targets for all three of these," Liladhar asked them.

"Yes, I think so. But then it will increase the complication to a much higher level," Anubhav said. "But, I liked the insight that you gave us about sales management. It has changed my perspective. I am also going to read the book, without fail."

"But, before that, you will have to do proper training of your entire sales teams so that all of them come on the same page regarding the concepts. Then you need to set targets for all these metrics. After that comes the question of measuring them," Liladhar said.

"Also, I suggest that you should use Data from the CRM tool to create the target management spreadsheets," Liladhar said. "What I mean to say is that you create all the formulas and templates in the spreadsheet. But link that spreadsheet to get the data from CRM. You will have to ask Bhamini from your CRM vendor team to help you with that," Liladhar said.

"Yes, I can do that. Once I do it for our team, I will share the structure with Irshad and Jagdeep also," Ramesh said.

"But using this system to manage sales forecast funnel and targets from spreadsheets would be too much of work for us," Jagdeep said.

"Sales forecast and Targets are different," Liladhar said.

Sales forecast and Sales Targets are different

"Target is something that is based on an organizational goal, on your aspiration. You want to achieve that," Liladhar explained. "The sales forecast is based on deals in hand and their probability of winning."

"It is effortless to get sales forecasts from your CRM system. There is a date field in the opportunity module called Expected Close Date (ECD). If all the salespeople fill up that field properly, then you have a very concrete sales forecast," Liladhar added.

"Ok, so for example, a total of all the opportunities having ECD, which is before the end of this month, will become the sales forecast for this month," Jagdeep asked.

"Exactly. This report is much more reliable than your spreadsheet since all the opportunities are real opportunities listed in the CRM. Also, the expected close dates are filled up by salespersons themselves, who are in constant contact with the prospects," Liladhar replied.

"If we allow salespersons to change ECD on their own, they will keep on postponing the date, and we will never have a reliable sales forecast," Ramesh showed his concern.

"I don't think so. If your sales managers are doing their duty properly, then this will never happen. Also, there is a mechanism in CRM to track all the changes that you do to that particular field," Liladhar said.

"However, I think we have to allow the salesperson to change the Expected Close Date, as per their gut feeling. Because they are in contact with the prospect, they know what is changing."

"Hmm, I get it. If we keep a daily track of the opportunities as we discussed previously, We can be sure of the sales forecast accuracy." Jagdeep said.

Sales targets v/s sales forecast.

Sales targets are something that you want to achieve; it is something that you aspire. They are based on organizational goals and ambition. In comparison, the sales forecast is based on the opportunities in hand and their probability of winning.

"I must say Liladhar; now we have a completely different picture of CRM than what we had before," Anubhav said. "It reminds me of a famous dialog from an Amitabh Bachchan movie called *Aankhen*, In which he had played the role of Vinay Singh Rajput. सच कल्पना से भी ज़्यादा विचित्र होता है. *(Truth is stranger than fiction)*."

"Yes, that's true. Today was a roller-coaster ride for all of us. You toppled lots of our beliefs and concepts. But it was beneficial," Ramesh said.

Liladhar had to go for his Ayurved and Yog classes. So, they all departed, to meet once again, maybe.

Chapter 5

Growing Your Business with CRM

छोटा जोखिम, छोटा फ़ायदा - उसे धंधा कहते है, बड़ा जोखिम, बड़ा फ़ायदा - उसे जुआ कहते है, छोटा जोखिम, बड़ा फ़ायदा - उसे मौक़ा कहते है

— Subhash (Paresh Rawal) in the Maharathi Movie.

It had been six months since they last met. All three friends of Liladhar were delighted with the CRM tool, It was implemented and used very nicely. So, Anubhav, Irshad, and Jagdeep wanted to give a special treat to Liladhar to thank him for helping and guiding them.

Of course, at the back of their mind, they also had the idea of getting some more pieces of practical advice which they can use to grow their business. Even though the CRM was implemented and adequately used now, they all thought that there could be vast hidden potential in the CRM platform, which they had not utilized.

They all wanted to uncover those hidden gems, which help them grow 10X and 100X, with the help of the CRM Technology and management principles shared by Liladhar.

This time, they met at The Orchid Hotel, in Vile Parle, Mumbai. As this was supposed to be a thanks-giving treat, Anubhav did not want anything to look mediocre.

Liladhar had landed in Mumbai after a long flight from London; it was early morning.

When Liladhar arrived at the restaurant, 'South Of Vindhyas, sharp at 8:30 am as decided, three of them were already waiting. They seemed more than happier.

"Here, they have India's best vegetarian breakfast," Anubhav flaunted once all of them settled on the table. "We specifically selected vegetarian as you don't eat non-veg."

"Sure, bring it on," Liladhar said. While they settled on the table, the discussion started with the usual small talk. That's when Liladhar asked them, "How is your CRM software working?."

"It's stranger than fiction. We are all enjoying it very much," Jagdeep said.

"Initially, we thought that the CRM would help us to monitor our teams. But in fact, it has changed our entire working style," Irshad added.

"Now we can say that our teams are in almost auto-mode," Anubhav said. It was like a dream come true for him. He no more had to do fire-fighting now. He did not get threatening escalation calls, but was well-informed of what was happening in his company by spending 20 minutes per day.

"Explain, please," Liladhar said as if he was teasing Jagdeep.

1. Creating a self-driven team with the help of CRM

"Before I tell you my story, I want to ask you one question. Our support team, who uses the ticketing system in our CRM, started to use it much faster. Their adoption was much quicker than our sales team. Why does that happen?" Irshad asked.

"Yes, even we had that experience," Anubhav added.

Why Support Teams adopt CRM faster than sales teams?

"This is natural. Your customers drive your Service team. The complaint reported by the customer triggers the action. If you don't provide the service, the customer will complain to the higher authorities," Liladhar explained.

"Now, consider, who is driving your sales team? What triggers the response by the Sales team?" Liladhar asked.

"The inquiries that we receive will trigger the sales team's response," Irshad replied. "However, many times, it is self-triggered."

"Maybe we can say that the sales team's actions are self-driven," Anubhav said.

"You are 100% right. We drive the sales team, and not the customer. Now, if we fail to follow up properly with the prospect, they might not even complain to the senior in your company," Liladhar said.

"Hmm. I get it now. As usual, you have proved that the problem lies on our side," Irshad said with a smirky smile.

"No, it is not like that, but the motivation matters. In fact, the same holds true for the accounts or the production team. Legal compliance drives the accounts team," Liladhar explained. "This is the reason you find that adoption in Accounts and inventory management software is always much better."

"That makes perfect sense. I never thought from that perspective," Irshad said.

"After our last meeting at Anubhav's office, we followed the policy of 'In God we trust, all others must bring data,' as said by William Edwards," Irshad started narrating his story.

"As you had rightly predicted, the biggest obstacles came from my partners and our senior sales team. In the beginning, I tried to persuade them as politely as I could. But beyond one point in time, I had to put my foot down," Irshad continued. "Initially, there were skirmishes, but as they started to see the benefits, they all started using the CRM. They also began following the processes properly," Irshad said. "The change not only happened in our sales team, but even our senior team has changed a lot."

CRM improves accountability, cross-team collaboration & Transparency

"The same is our case now, I think. My entire company is working effortlessly. We now don't have stormy meetings and stressful sales reviews," Anubhav added.

"And how did that happen?" Liladhar asked.

"now we all use the owner-notification system very effectively. Every day morning, all the team leaders check the CRM dashboard. Which means they are updated every day about the sales funnel," Anubhav said. "I think this is the main reason why our sales team also started to use the CRM very effectively. Now, they get all the help from their seniors, even before their working day begins," Anubhav said.

"My dad used to say -'All the changes have to begin at the top. Most people are not bad, but they are waiting for someone to lead them properly,'" Liladhar said in a philosophical tone.

"I must say one more thing. Now the accountability and cross-department collaboration have increased significantly," Anubhav said.

"Initially, when a salesperson needed a technical support person, he used to go to his team leader, who, in turn would discuss with the tech support head. Then the Tech support head is used to allocate the resources. This took us a very long time to respond," Anubhav said.

"How has that changed now?" Liladhar asked.

"Now, salespersons just raise a ticket for the demo to be done. That ticket is allocated to the service team head, who will assign it to his team member. The work gets done very quickly, as all of this happens on the mobile CRM app," Anubhav said with a winning smile. "The best part is that I get to see all this action in my team on my mobile CRM app," Anubhav added.

"We made a tiny change in visits (activity) module to accommodate conveyance charges and other expenditure. So now our sales team does not have to create vouchers to claim the expenses. Also, now Jaspreet, my wife, who handles finance, can approve the expenditure from the CRM software itself," Jagdeep said.

"Also, Jaspreet does not have to ask questions regarding why that expense was made. Everything is visible to her in the CRM itself. This has reduced unnecessary communication loops that used to happen before," Jagdeep added.

"Using business process software is like joining the Gym. It takes time for changes to be visible, but after some time, the benefits become evident. Also, the speed of change increases significantly," Liladhar said.

"Maybe because of the increased transparency and automation, I don't know. But now I see much better accountability and a sense of responsibility within the team," Anubhav said.

"I must tell you one thing," Liladhar said. "The food is awesome here. We should have arranged all the meetings at this place."

"We are glad that you enjoyed it. We could not think of this place, maybe because we were so confused with the CRM challenges," Anubhav said.

"आफ़त में अवसर होता है, *(There is always an opportunity in the adversity)*. I am glad that you all could make a significant change in your organization. All because you used the system effectively," Liladhar said.

"No, I think it is because of your guidance. All CRM vendors tell us what features their CRM has, but no one tells us what we have to do. That I think is the reason why almost all the companies are in a permanent struggle with CRM."

"Yes, your experience and practical knowledge helped us to crack this code of CRM. We are feeling like we have solved some impossible puzzle. It was because of your help. We could use the CRM to its maximum level," Jagdeep said with gratitude.

"But, the game is not over yet. It has just begun. What makes you think that you have reached maximum utilization of CRM?" Liladhar asked them.

"What? What other benefits can we get from CRM? We would certainly like to know and implement them in our companies," Anubhav said. He seemed super excited.

 Some hidden benefits of CRM.

A CRM tool, when appropriately implemented, significantly improves teamwork, accountability, collaboration, and transparency. The benefits are much beyond the software functions.

"There are many things that you can do. Let us discuss a few of them, which I think are very important," Liladhar said. "But let me finish this filter coffee; it's awesome."

After finishing their heavenly breakfast, they moved to a quieter coffee shop in the same hotel to continue their discussion. They were going to spend their whole day in The Orchid, as Anubhav had planned the lunch also in the same place.

2. What can the marketing team learn by analyzing CRM data?

"Now that your teams have started using CRM effectively, the first thing it can help you do is improve your sales and marketing processes," Liladhar said.

Improve sales qualification processes using the learnings from lost deals

"When you lose the deals or opportunities as some people call them, you also define the reason for losing the sale," Liladhar said.

"Yes, we do. We are doing it religiously," Jagdeep said.

"What do you learn from that?" Liladhar asked.

"We come to know why we lose sales, and what we can do about it?" Jagdeep replied.

"And what do you do with that knowledge?" Liladhar asked.

"As such nothing. That makes us aware of the market condition and our competitiveness," Jagdeep replied.

"We also discuss the same in our meetings. If there are some mistakes from our side, we make sure that we avoid them in the future," Anubhav added. "What else can we do with that data?"

"If you properly analyze the reasons for losing the sales, in many cases, you will find that you could have been able to predict the fate of the deal, provided you had some information about the deal in the initial stage?" Liladhar said.

"With this knowledge, we can change our inquiry qualification process. So that we don't waste the efforts of our sales team on those deals," Liladhar continued.

"Explain, please," Jagdeep said.

"Let me give you an elementary example. In my company, we observed that when we got an inquiry from Tax consultants for our Task Management software in our earlier days. They found the software very good. Still, eventually, they would seldom buy it," Liladhar said.

"After thorough investigation, we figured out that all those tax consultants who also provided financial services to their clients found our software to be lacking a few modules for that particular business vertical," Liladhar continued.

"So what did you do?" Jagdeep asked.

"Working on those deals was a wasteful exercise for us, which could have been avoided. Also, it left a horrible impression on our clients' minds that we did not have the required features. Whereas what they demanded was not in our roadmap," Liladhar added.

"We could have easily known in the initial phase of the inquiry that they also offered financial services. We just had to ask them some more questions," Liladhar said.

"So we changed our sales qualification process and started asking our prospective customers whether they offered financial services or not. If they provided, then we disqualified those inquiries. This saved a huge amount of time and money for us."

"That's interesting. Now, I realize that even for our projects, a lot of efforts are currently getting wasted. We have to do a POC (Proof of concept) and Demo, which are very costly in terms of time and human resources," Anubhav said.

"There is one more thing that you can learn from the deals," Liladhar said. "It will help you to improve your marketing effectiveness."

Create customer persona for marketing

"But we don't do any marketing, and we don't have a marketing department," Jagdeep said.

"I disagree. You may not have a department, but you definitely do marketing activities. You have a website, visiting cards, brochures; you attend events. All of these are marketing activities," Liladhar said.

"The secret to make your marketing activities effective is to know who your customer is. As they call in marketing jargon, create a customer persona," Liladhar said.

"What is the customer persona, and how do we create that?" Jagdeep asked.

"Customer persona is a hypothetical character of your ideal customer. Having a properly defined customer persona helps you focus your marketing efforts," Liladhar said. "You can analyze deals closed to get data regarding your customers and why they bought from you. Apart from primary classification like Industry and vertical, you can collect much more critical information, like systems they use, the products they offer, or maybe machines that they have," Liladhar continued.

"To create a proper customer persona, you may also capture, what are actual pain or challenges of your customers that you solve," Liladhar added.

Make your marketing effective with learnings from dead leads

"You all are using inquiry modules, and then you qualify them and convert them to opportunities. If they don't qualify, then you mark them as dead. Is that how it works for you?" Liladhar asked.

"Yes, perfectly correct," Irshad nodded.

"If you analyze the dead inquiries, there are chances that you find the problem with your marketing activity. Maybe with the perception that the market has regarding you," Liladhar said.

"Let me speak on behalf of Jagdeep this time. Explain, please," Irshad said with an innocently wicked smile.

"A few years back, we launched a telephony product, a smart PBX, with a lot more features than regular PBX. A PBX device operates your internal telephone lines and connects them to external lines. The launch was successful; we received more than 500 inquiries. But even after 45 days, there was not a single sale," Liladhar said.

"Also, most of the inquiries were turning dead. The reason that everyone was giving us was that our product was costly," Liladhar continued. "Out of 500 plus, our sales team disqualified nearly 480 of the inquiries."

"But what was the actual problem?" Jagdeep was curious.

"We found that people were finding our solution costly because they were comparing it with the low-cost PBXs in the market," Liladhar revealed. "The actual problem was that on our website and in all email marketing also, we had mentioned our new product as an economical alternative to PBX."

"Whereas it should have been an intelligent alternative to PBX," Liladhar said. "Then, we changed the content and reran the marketing campaign. This time, we got fewer inquiries, but the conversion rate was significantly higher than before."

"That was very insightful; I will have to check this in my company too. I am sure that we will be able to optimize our marketing efforts to a great extent," Anubhav said.

"These ideas will only apply to larger organizations like Anubhav's. How can it apply to smaller companies like ours," Jagdeep asked.

"Why not? Did you realize that your brand and your marketing is done by your sales and service teams when they meet or greet your clients?" Liladhar asked. "Just listen to how your team does a self-introduction. Even if you listen to the way your salesperson speaks, then you will get to know a lot of insights," Liladhar said, without waiting for an answer from Jagdeep.

"By the way, the cheapest way to increase sales without spending a bomb on marketing is by doing cross-selling and up-selling. Your CRM can help you a lot to implement that process and culture."

Jagdeep said, "Explain, please."

"One day, I am going to ask Jaspreet how many times in a day you tell her these words. Explain, please," Anubhav said mischievously.

"Before I answer that, I want all of you to understand one thing," Liladhar said in a rather severe tone.

"Yes, please go ahead. We are all ears," Anubhav said.

"I need a coffee to go ahead," Liladhar said, as it was not his turn to play mischief on Anubhav.

3. How to implement the Cross-Selling process and culture?

"If cross-selling and upselling is implemented properly across the team, then that would be the secret to grow 10X without much effort," Liladhar said.

"You all are aware of what is cross-selling and upselling, right?" Liladhar asked.

"Of course, when we sell a complementary or related product to our existing customers, it is called cross-selling.," Jagdeep replied.

"Upselling is when we sell the same product to the same customer, but in more quantity or more frequently," Irshad replied. It felt like they were answering their teacher in their classroom.

"Now, for small businesses, cross-selling and upselling are the cheapest way to increase the sales and profitability without burning a hole in the pocket," Liladhar said.

"I understand that it will increase sales, but how does it increase profitability?" Jagdeep asked.

"When you make the first sale to any customer, 80% of your effort goes in winning the trust of the customer that they can buy from you. The remaining 20% is required to sell the product. So, when you sell them a product, you already have the trust. Now, you just have to convince the customer to buy another product," Liladhar continued. "That is the reason that your sales effort reduces, thereby reducing your costs," Liladhar concluded.

"Also, you generally get better margins and payment terms from your existing customers," Anubhav added.

"My personal experience says that upselling is much more beneficial than cross-selling because there you don't even have to make much effort to sell the product. Your customer is already using that product. You just sell more quantity of it. It's a repeat order," Irshad added.

"Exactly!" Liladhar added.

"Now, all of you personally know how to practice cross-selling and upselling. The problem is that each one of your salespeople might not be practicing it," Liladhar added. "Which means that we don't have a process and culture of cross-selling."

"Yes. In fact, the problem gets aggravated when you have different teams selling different products," Anubhav added from his *anubhav.*

"So we need to create processes and culture that will foster cross-selling and upselling," Liladhar said.

"Bhamini, our CRM success officer from our CRM Vendor, had informed us that there is a cross-selling module in the CRM. But we have never explored it," Anubhav said.

"Yes, but the tool is not important; it's the practice and mindset of cross-selling, which is critical," Liladhar said. "The tool is straightforward."

"A CRM allows you to configure the categories of offerings that you have for your customers. Your offerings include your product and service categories. Then for every customer, you select the status of the product for the customer," Liladhar said.

Using CRM for cross-selling

"Let us consider the example of Anubhav. They sell Desktops, Servers, Networking, security, and Cloud. That makes five offerings," Liladhar continued.

"But we have many types of gears. Can we make as many categories as we want?" Jagdeep asked.

"Yes, you can, but that is not advisable. Remember, we are defining categories, not products. You should have a maximum of 5 or six. Otherwise, the entire purpose of this exercise gets defeated," Liladhar explained. "You will come to know why I am telling this."

"Now, for every customer, you have to select the status for each of the products. There can be five possible statuses, *Not required, Sold, not pitched, Upsell, In the process.*"

"Wait, wait. It sounds very confusing. Please draw on this paper," Irshad requested, while he handed over his diary with a new page opened on it.

Liladhar drew a table similar to the one below:

Customer Name	Desktop	Servers	Networking	Security	Cloud
Customer 1					
Customer 2					
Customer 3					

Five stages:

1. No Need- You approached the customer, but they didn't need it.

2. Sold - Already sold. Not possible to sell more.

3. Not Pitched - You have not tried approaching the customer for this product.

4. Upsell - You have already sold the product, and there is a possibility of selling more.

5. In process - the deal for this product is already in-process.

"Now it is much more clear. But who will fill up this data?" Irshad asked.

"That is the catch. This is not the format of data; it is the format of the discussion," Liladhar explained.

Jagdeep was going to say something, and all three smiled at him.

"I will explain!" Liladhar said.

"Different team members might be handling different products or customers. They have information about the customer, the products they have bought, and what else they might buy," Liladhar said.

"So this table brings all of that information together," Anubhav said.

"Exactly! You are already doing sales review meetings every week. I would suggest you include a cross-selling meeting, in the same meeting," Liladhar said.

Liladhar continued, "Let us say that you ask each salesperson to write their one or two customers and then discuss what products they have bought and what other products we can pitch."

"Whatever is the opinion of the salesperson, we will write it and fill it up in the CRM," Liladhar said. "Eventually, this table will get filled up, and it might look something like this."

Customer Name	Desktop	Servers	Networking	Security	Cloud
Customer 1	Sold	UpSell	Not Pitched	Sold	No Need
Customer 2	Not Pitched	Sold	No Need	UpSell	In-Process
Customer 3	UpSell	UpSell	In-Process	Not Pitched	UpSell

"I hope now it makes some sense to all of you," Liladhar asked.

"No, it does not make some sense," Anubhav said with a mischievous smile. "Actually, it makes a lot of sense. This can be a game-changer for us," Anubhav showed his excitement.

"I want you to notice something here," Liladhar said. "*Sold* and *No Need* means you don't have to do anything there. Even for entries about deals in hand, you don't have to do anything special. Your team is already following up," Liladhar added.

Liladhar continued with a spark in his eyes, "However, Upsell and In-Process show the highest potential opportunities. In fact, you just created new opportunities for yourself, without any extra cost or effort."

"But we have hundreds of customers. This means a lot of work," Irshad said.

"Is that a big problem or a huge opportunity?" Liladhar asked. "Don't you want lots of leads?"

"Yes, I agree. If we do it regularly, we will have doubled our sales in the next 12 months. Also, my sales team will have a great funnel to work on," Irshad concluded.

"Hold your excitement; I want to warn you against potential failure points," Liladhar said.

Precautions to take while implementing cross-selling

"What are they?"

"Firstly, this is a team exercise. If you have a team, please don't assign it to any one person; otherwise, it will fail," Liladhar continued.

"I have a question. Can we use this for services as well?" Irshad asked. "As we also sell maintenance contracts and services to our customers. Contracts and services are good sources of income for us."

"Yes, of course," Liladhar said.

"Another point to keep in mind is that you should not try to analyze all customers in one meeting. Go slow and steady, give proper thought, and discuss it in detail with your salespeople. Discuss each client thoroughly," Liladhar added.

"What should we do when there is an *upsell* opportunity? I mean, how do we track and follow it up?" Irshad asked.

"Just create an opportunity in the CRM immediately. Do it in the sales review meeting itself so that you don't miss it," Liladhar said.

"By that logic, I think we should create a lead for *not pitched* items," Jagdeep added.

"Yes, you are right," Liladhar said. "Just make sure that you update the cross-selling information when the lead is converted, or the deal is closed. This will keep your cross-selling information up to date and relevant.

"The best way to keep up the practice is to discuss the clients, which you got in the last one week or one month. Since they are new clients, your sales team will already have a lot of information about the customer fresh in their memories.

"I think that the Cross-selling idea that we discussed today is going to help all of us to a great extent," Irshad said.

"Just remember one thing. Don't overdo it. Don't complicate things. Otherwise, instead of using CRM, you will all fall in the technical trap of CRM," Liladhar warned them.

"Anyone for a quick round of a hot coffee?" Anubhav asked, and then without waiting for an answer, he ordered the filter coffee, as Liladhar liked it. "We also have a special guest who is coming now for a coffee with us."

"Who is coming?" Jagdeep asked with curiosity?

"Someone we have to thank," Anubhav said, raising the suspense.

"Ah, there he is," Anubhav got up from his seat as a gentleman approached them.

The fifth person joined them at the table. Anubhav introduced him, "Friends, meet Mr. Abhimanyu Rai, CEO of Sangam CRM, the person behind the company who has provided the CRM."

Jagdeep, Anubhav, and Irshad had bought the CRM solution from Abhimanyu's company.

"Hi Abhimanyu, good to see you after a long time," Liladhar greeted Abhimanyu. It seemed like both of them knew each other for a long time.

Anubhav, Jagdeep, and Irshad looked confused, "Liladhar, do you know each other?"

Abhimanyu interrupted, "Can I reply, Sir? Actually, I was working for Mr. Liladhar Shastri for the initial five years of my life. Then I left to start my own business."

"I am glad you started the business and followed your passion," Liladhar said.

"So, for the last ten years, we have been helping businesses to manage their sales and service teams, with our CRM," Abhimanyu said.

"I must tell you that your CRM software is too good. But your team is the best. They are very proactive and always enthusiastic about helping your clients," Anubhav said.

"Everything I have learned from Liladhar Sir," Abhimanyu said with all the gratitude in his eyes.

"Liladhar, I have one question. Which CRM are you using? Are you not using Sangam CRM, from Abhimanyu's company?" Jagdeep asked.

"How can I use something else? In fact, I was the first customer to go for Sangam CRM," Liladhar said.

"More than a customer! Sir has been instrumental in teaching my team and me how to do business. He helped us formulate almost all our processes," Abhimanyu said.

"So, we all are using Sangam CRM. Why did you not tell us about Abhimanyu before? It would have avoided all the trouble in evaluating and buying CRM," Anubhav complained.

"There were two reasons. First, I did not want to influence your decision and ask you to give the order to Abhimanyu just because I knew him," Liladhar said.

"Second, I wanted you to understand the process and go through that journey. Otherwise, we would not have been sitting here to celebrate your success," Liladhar added.

Just then, the waiter arrived with a tray of coffee and some cookies.

4. CRM is the SME's secret weapon to fight giant MNCs

"I am happy that my CRM Solution has been able to help you to run your businesses," Abhimanyu Rai said. Even though he was the CEO of a successful company, he didn't look like one. He was humble and modest, traits similar to his mentor Liladhar Shastri.

"Abhimanyu, there are many CRM vendors in India. Most of them are large corporations with deep pockets. What is your opinion about small business owners' chances of survival in this scenario," Jagdeep asked Abhimanyu.

"I ask because all of us are facing similar challenges from larger companies, especially MNCs, who sometimes have predatory practices," Jagdeep continued. "Since you are doing it successfully, I want to know your experience and perspective on this."

"The key is a world-class customer experience. Both in sales and service," Abhimanyu replied.

"I agree that larger companies have lots of money and technology. But as a small business owner, we have one thing that they cannot have. It is our relationships with our customers," Abhimanyu said. "But relationships alone will not make us competitive; we will need technology to help us, especially for managing sales teams," Abhimanyu added.

"Also, I think that the biggest problem of SMEs is not lack of funds. But it is the lack of a professional sales team," Abhimanyu continued.

"So, you are helping small business owners to fight their battle of survival and also grow?" Jagdeep asked and said at the same time.

"We are lucky to be in the right place at the right time so that we get the chance to serve our customers. In fact, we are all in the best times. Primarily because of cloud and mobile technology. These two things have democratized costly technology and made it available for everyone at a small recurring cost.

"It's an opportunity for all of us to grow. Liladhar Sir, remember, you used to tell us one Hindi movie dialogue, which is regarding the opportunity," Abhimanyu asked.

"Ah yes, There was a movie called *Maharathi*, which literally means a supreme warrior. Paresh Rawal, the great actor, played the role of Subhash Kumar in that movie. The movie had a dialog, which goes like this"

छोटा जोखिम, छोटा फ़ायदा - उसे धंधा कहते है,

बड़ा जोखिम, बड़ा फ़ायदा - उसे जुआ कहते है,

छोटा जोखिम, बड़ा फ़ायदा - उसे मौक़ा कहते है

"In English, it means, *Small Risk, Small Reward; is called Business. Big Risk, Big Reward; is called Gambling. Small Risk, Big Reward, is called Opportunity,"* Liladhar said.

"So, investing in a proper sales process and CRM is a small risk and big reward. It's an opportunity," Liladhar said.

"Let's raise a toast for the opportunity called life," Anubhav said, as they all raised their coffee.

Printed in Great Britain
by Amazon

16674192R00093